The Black American History Edition

BLACK MASSACRES

Written and Organized

by

Maham the Mentor

i

BLACK MASSACRES

Publisher's Cataloging-in-Publication data
Names: Maham the Mentor, author.
Title: Black massacres : a tribute to Black Wall Street , the Black massacre in Tulsa , Oklahoma / by
Maham the Mentor.
Description: Includes index. | Dallas, TX: Maham the Mentor Books, LLC., 2022.
Identifiers: LCCN: 2022915309 | ISBN: 979-8-9860422-0-6
Subjects: LCSH African Americans--Oklahoma--Tulsa--History--20th century. | Racism--Oklahoma--Tulsa--
History--20th century. | Riots--Oklahoma--Tulsa--History--20th century. | Tulsa Race Massacre, Tulsa,
Okla., 1921. | Violence--Oklahoma--Tulsa--History--20th century. | African American neighborhoods--
Oklahoma--Tulsa--History--20th century. | Tulsa (Okla.)--Race relations. | BISAC HISTORY / African
American & Black | HISTORY / United States / 20th Century | HISTORY / United States / State & Local /
Southwest (AZ, NM, OK, TX)
Classification: LCC F704.T92 .M34 2022 | DDC 976.6/8600496073--dc23

MAHAM THE MENTOR

TRIBUTION

A Tribute to Black Wall Street,
The Tulsa, Oklahoma Massacre.
The 27 Black Massacres in America
After the Civil War began.

MAHAM THE MENTOR

CONTENTS

MAHAM THE MENTOR

MAHAM THE MENTOR

INTRODUCTION

Maham the Mentor
A Tribute to Black Wall Street, The Tulsa, Oklahoma Massacre.
The 27 Black Massacres that happened in America After the Civil War began.

      Today's date is May 31st, 2021. The Official 100 years Anniversary of Black Wall Street. The Black Massacre in Tulsa, Oklahoma in 1921. There's wisdom and knowledge in the most unfortunate places. We should know our past to appreciate our future. As an Educated Black man in America, I'm aware of the impact and the importance of having the knowledge of our history. Having the knowledge of the History of Black People in America is great for All Races when it is explained right. Which is why I have taken it upon myself to write a series of Books on Black American History. As a strong Black Man. I can honestly say, I love this country and I appreciate this country. My country is my extended family. Our America School systems have failed us on Black History. Less than 10% of class time is devoted to Black History. Only 8% of Seniors can identify slavery as a main cause of the Civil War. Each State must decide on what the students will learn. Seven of our States don't even mention Slavery in their History lessons (Alaska, Montana, Wyoming, Iowa, Maine, Vermont, and Rhode Island.) Eight of our States don't mention the Civil Rights movement. (Alaska, Oregon, Montana, Wyoming, South Dakota, Missouri, Rhode Island, and Maine) Only two States Mention White Supremacy. (Massachusetts and Maryland). There are no National Standards for Black History. No plans for one. But in 2021, in America. We are passing Laws to limit Critical Race Theories for fear of people condemning white people. Because how we tell Black People, Black History is extremely important, especially when so many lies and stereotypes running rampant. We must remember our past to truly appreciate our future. As Black people, our History in America has kind of been whitewashed, which led many to believe that Black people had no value and played no real role in building America. So much Black American History is missing from America History, it devalues the many Black people who sacrifice their lives for our freedom. No Love or Respect for those people. As today marks, The 100 Year Anniversary of Black Wall Street. Many young Black Americans are totally oblivious to the realization that the Black Wall Street is just One in 27 Black Massacres that has happened after the Civil War began. The Black Wall Street is one of the last Black Massacres that occurred in America. It's just 100 years old today. The time is now. I feel it's my responsibility to educate all Human beings about Black American History, especially my young Black Men and women. I plan to continue to produce more books in

BLACK MASSACRES

line with this one. Black American History is so Rich. There's so much to learn and so much to teach. Where to begin and where to end. Since, there's no right or wrong answers. I'm starting off with Black Massacres in America, after the Civil War began. Because before that; it was basically legal. So, no one was really documenting those events. The 1921 Black Massacres of Tulsa, Oklahoma. Better known as Black Wall Street was one of the last Black Massacres in America's History. Sadly, to say. Most of Americans don't know this fact. Going through these horrific events that happened here in the Land of the free and the home of the brave. I hope to enlighten us all about the real adversity Black people went through for us all to have the opportunity to have a Life, Liberty, and the pursuit of Property or the pursuit of happiness. Without Black people, there would be no America. I know and understand this to the fullest. So, I sincerely thank all the Black people who have died before me, playing their part in establishing this great Nation. Since the beginning of this country, Black people have always been the cornerstone of this society, Black people built it, period. It is that simple. "The Land in America in 1619 was unmanageable to work for white people". America's beginning time places us in Jamestown, Virginia. It was too hard for white people to work that land. Black labor was the only thing that gave the land any Value. Without that, nothing happens (Condé Nast. "James Baldwin: Letter from a Region in My Mind." The New Yorker, 10 Nov. 1962). 1619 is way before the industrial revolution that happened in the 1900s, meaning. There were no manufacturing plants or factories of this period. Everyone, everywhere had to work in the fields, agriculture was the way of life back then. Many educators claim or teach that Black people in America started in the Transatlantic Slave trade. Which is during the years of 1526-1808 AD. I believe that it started in the year 711 AD. When Black People from North Africa enslaved White people in Spain and Portugal and kept them enslaved for 700 years. I'll explain more about that later in my book called when The Black People (Moors) enslaved the White People in Spain and Portugal. Let's get into these Black Massacres.

REFERENCE

Condé Nast. "James Baldwin: Letter from a Region in My Mind." The New Yorker, 10 Nov. 1962,
https://www.newyorker.com/magazine/1962/11/17/letter-from-a-region-in-my-mind.

CHAPTER ONE
THE FIRST BLACK MASSACRE.
NEW YORK CITY 1863.

The First Black Massacre that happened after the Civil War started, was covered up with the name, "the New York City Draft Riots", it occurred on July 11, 1863 – July 16, 1863, which is right in the middle of the Civil War. Many things we already know about New York City. And here's the things they don't really teach. Most Americans will know that the U.S. Civil War was the most violent Insurrection in U.S. history. But the second most violent Insurrection came during the Civil War, and no one really knows about it.

Well, kind of, in the year 2002, a movie called "Gangs of New York" was made. This movie was made, not to show people the truth. But to brush over it. Why do I say that? Well, the movie was based in New York City in 1863, these gangs are real. Dead Rabbits were Extremely Racist Irish immigrants. The Nativist Protestant were also extremely racist, too. But also hated white immigrants as well. This movie was not made behind the Thousands of Black People who were murdered in cold blood by white ignorant people in New York City and the white people who were never brought to justice. This movie was made to honor the white people who died. But you can see the aftermath. This movie takes the focus off the real issue and puts it on the gangs. But the real issue in New York City in 1863 wasn't the gangs at all, it was the Black people.

This insurrection, like Jan 6, 2021, kind of hidden away in history, still says much about the tensions between the Black and white races. The 1863 New York City draft riots, which turned into the First Black Massacre are history that deserves to be remembered. When the first shots of the Civil

1

BLACK MASSACRES

War were fired in the attack on Fort Sumter in April of 1861, few in the Nation could anticipate how destructive the war would be, but any illusions of a war being easily won were lost in 1862. As the battle of Shiloh became

the deadliest battle in the history of the Nation. Only to be topped later in the same year by the battle of Antietam. Still the bloodiest day in the history of the United States. President Abraham Lincoln issued the Emancipation Proclamation in January 1863 it really was just a war tactic. The major purpose was to keep European Nations from entering the war on behalf of the Confederacy and destroy their free-labor work force also called slavery. But the devastation of war went on. The battle of Chancellorsville topped Antietam, as the bloodiest battle in the Nation's history; and then was itself topped in the long three-day Battle of Gettysburg, Fought from July First to the third. In New York the Nation's biggest city, the war only highlighted underlying tensions between the races. The city had been the epicenter of mass immigration in the first half of the 19th century. Prior to 1830, nearly all population growth in the US was internal and 98% of the population was native born" (Contributors to Wikimedia projects. "Padang Galo - Wikipedia." Wikimedia Foundation, Inc., 26 Apr. 2021).

In the decade between 1820 and 1830, around 140,000 white people immigrated to the U.S. In the decade between 1850 and 1860, that number had grown to 1.7 million the foreign born. Population in the United States had nearly doubled between the 1850 and the 1860. Census say Irish immigration made up almost 40% at the foreign-born population in 1860 Germans almost a third. Some 90% of the mass immigration of the antebellum period came North. As new immigrants could not compete with the free labor of southern slaves, and it was northern cities that were the most transformed. By 1860, nearly half of the population of New York City was foreign born. This mass migration resulted in inevitable fight and fate of this backlash. In New York the rival white Street Gangs of the Nativist Bowery Boys and the Irish Dead Rabbits had led to a violent confrontation in 1857, called the Dead Rabbits riot. That resulted in eight deaths and required the intervention of the New York State militia to restore order. The attention also affected New York City politics. Where the Democrat machine of Tammany Hall, actively recruited immigrant populations. Whereas the Abolitionists were often anti-immigrant bigots. The anti-immigrant knows nothing party, had gained political clout in the 1850s. And politics in New York City began to be defined by immigrant and anti-immigrant factions.

A white racist Democrat named Fernando Wood had been elected to a second term as Mayor of New York City in 1860. Supported strongly by the Dead Rabbits, Wood, was one of the Democratic Copperheads, who opposed the war, and was sympathetic to the southern racist cause. In 1861, he appealed to the city's board of Alderman for New York to secede from the Union and declare itself a free city. Although the Council balked at his suggestion, it might seem contradictory that the Abolitionists were the

nativists; and the relatively proslavery Democrats were the party of immigrants. But the economics made sense. The economy of New York City was tied to exports. And prior to the Civil War, nearly half of those exports were southern cotton, and the revenues those exports earned is what funded the patronage. It supported the Democratic Party machine. Mayor Wood quoted the immigrant books. Ordering, that New Yorkers, should take care of its own working class before fighting a war over the working class of other states. In the face of increasingly vocal Abolitionists in the city of Democrats. It inflamed their Irish and German immigrants to hate Black freedom. More Reports of people claiming that abolition would cause an influx of new Black freedmen to the city who would compete for labor. To these white immigrants, already living in poverty and crowded slums. The Emancipation Proclamation had been the realization of their fears. Meanwhile, the Union had suffered a string of defeats and reverses in the first two years of the Civil War. And the News Press was increasingly defeatist as hope for a quick victory had given way to the reality of the terrible fight. Even as the Union army needed new recruits to make good, its losses had shifted the tide of the wars voluntary enlistments had plummeted. In March 1863 Congress had passed the enrollment Act. A form of National conscription intended to replenish the ranks of the Union Army. The Act required the enrollment of every white male citizen and those immigrants who had filed for citizenship between the ages of 20 and 45. White men would then be drafted, by law, free to meet enlistment quotas. The Act included a provision that was intended to soften opposition which became particularly controversial. A white person drafted could avoid service if they could find a substitute, a person paid to take their place or pay a commutation of $300. As most working individuals could not afford such a fee that meant that the Act disproportionately affected the working class; and gave rise to the slogan rich man's war poor man's fight. The Act further contributed to the tension over labor as Black Men were not subject to the Act. At this time Black people were not yet considered citizens. Anti-war or white racist newspapers worked to inflame the sentiment in the months between the passage of the Act and the first draft lotteries decrying the fact that the $300 commutation was a third the average price of a slave in the South. Making a working white man, less valuable than a Black slave. The first round of draft numbers occurred in New York City in July of 1863. Less than two weeks after the bloody Union victory at the Battle of Gettysburg. In a city that was seething with tensions over class and race. The first drawing of 1200 names on July 11th went peacefully enough. The city seed over the next day and the powder keg erupted. When the second drawing names began on Monday the 13th, at US Provo Marshalls enrollment office at 3rd Ave and 47th St. A white rowdy crowd gathered and as more names started to be drawn, suddenly a gunshot rang out. As if on cue, the mob of white people started attacking the office with paving stones. And trying to storm the building to destroy the enrollment documents sound familiar? Lol. Setting the building on fire. When the Volunteer Fire Department tried to fight the fires. The White Mob attacked them and destroyed their equipment. Other white people attacked streetcars killing the horses and breaking up the cars. Then they tore down the Telegraph lines to prevent communication to the rest of the city. As the rioting spread the Metropolitan Police department tried to quell the violence but their force was outnumbered. The New York State militia had been sent to the great battle at Gettysburg. Leaving the city virtually undefended. When the police Superintendent John Kennedy arrived to assess the situation. The White crown attacked him and brutally beat him. While they were unable to quell riots. The police had some success containing them. When the mob attacked the office of the New York Tribune, A permanent republican and ambitious newspaper with the intent of hanging editor Horace Greeley. A group of nearly 100 officers attacked the mob from the rear. Causing them to clear the building. The staff members of the New York Times turned the White mob back, themselves by manning gatling guns. The White mob targeted homes of draft supporters; well-known Republicans; and the wealthy. On 5th Ave, the White Mob went looting as they set fire to the 8th and 5th district police stations. The largely White Irish Catholic rioters targeted the Protestant charities. Such as, the Magdalene Asylum and the Five Points Mission. When the management of the Bulls Head Hotel on 44th Street refused to serve them alcohol. They burned the hotel to the ground. The White mob brutally targeted Black People. The mob's mission was to try to eradicate Black People from the labor force. They especially targeted Black workers near the docks. Where they have been seen as the biggest threat to

4

good labor for white folks. Black Men were beaten, stabbed, and lynched in the streets. And their bodies mutilated. Businesses that serve Black patrons were burned down to the ground. The white crowd burned the pharmacy owned by James McKune Smith. On West Broadway, thought to be the first Black owned pharmacy in America. The white mob targeted the Colored orphan asylum on 5th Ave between 43rd and 45th streets. A symbol of White charity towards Blacks and Black upward mobility. The police and staff were able to evacuate the 223 children. But the White mob looted and burned the building and savagely beat a White Irishman who tried to intervene on behalf of the children. The White Mob continued looting converting through the next day. By Wednesday troops hastily set from Pennsylvania started to arrive. By Thursday thousands of federal troops were in the city, the white mob militia continued to skirmish, but troops had the upper hand. A final confrontation on the night of the 16th, killed a dozen people.

In all about 120 people were killed In the New York City Black Massacre. Most all of them Black Men. At least eleven Black Men were lynched in the streets. Thousands of Black People were injured, and property damage was estimated between one to $5 million. The equivalent of roughly 20 to 100 million in today's dollars. In all, 50 buildings were destroyed in the Black Massacre. Some historians have considered the actions by these white people and the amount of damage done there was like a Confederate victory on the battlefield. 67 people were tried and convicted for crimes committed during the Black Massacre, but largely did not see long sentences. Lincoln reduced the draft quotas for New York City by almost half as a result of this Black Massacre. The tensions that drove the Black Massacre largely reduced afterwards. It became clear, quickly, that the draft was not going to affect nearly as many people as once thought. And that it didn't disproportionately affect working class white people. Because the Union had a reason to protect its industrial labor force. Former anti-immigrant Unionist started to embrace immigration as a way of increasing both the industrial potential and the available pool of manpower during the war. Some 200,000 German immigrants and 140,000 Irish immigrants fought for the Union during the Civil War. The former anti-immigrant Unionist saw them as actually having earned their place in the Nation because of their service. By the end of the 19th century anti-immigrant racism had become focused on immigrants from China. With European immigrants being seen as more benign. Sympathy for the Confederate causes slowly faded in New York State. Which eventually contributed more than 450,000 troops to the Union cause during the Civil War. In the end, the biggest impact of the 1863 New York City, Black

BLACK MASSACRES

Massacre was on the Black population of Manhattan. While there were several relief organizations who try to provide relief to victims of the Black massacre. Black people were understandably reticent to return to Manhattan after the violence. Property owners were reticent to lease to Black tenants for fear of reprisals. Manhattan, which prior to the Civil War, had seen one of the biggest populations of Black freedmen areas in America. Black population decrease by more than 20%. When the Colored orphanage asylum was eventually rebuilt. It was rebuilt on what was at the time the very outskirts of the city. The white working class again took control of the workforce. Continuing discrimination and Jim Crow laws eventually caused what was called the great migration of Black people to New York City after the war. They mostly relocated to the new Harlem neighborhood. While the immigrant tensions that were part of the Black Massacre had largely decreased. The racial tensions which underlie the 1863 Black Massacre had not been resolved. In fact, those issues are still here and they still impact the city and the Nation today. The 1863 New York City Black Massacre changed the city forever. And it also challenged that perception, that the Civil War was somehow a fight between a supposedly enlightened North and a racist South. It is history that deserves to be remembered in the history as the First Black Massacres, some could even say, it was worst then Black Wall Street.

REFERENCE

Contributors to Wikimedia projects. "Padang Galo - Wikipedia." Wikimedia Foundation, Inc., 26 Apr. 2021, https://en.wikipedia.org/wiki?curid=4647311

CHAPTER TWO
THE SECOND BLACK MASSACRE.
MEMPHIS, TN 1866.

The Memphis Black Massacre of 1866, in the city of Memphis, TN started from May 1st to May 3rd, 1866. Over one year after the U.S. Civil War ended. 48 men were dead. 46 of whom were Black freedmen. And most of them being veterans of the union army. 70 more wounded, five Black women were raped, 91 homes, 12 churches, and four schools were burned down. By the end of it, over $17,000 in federal property was destroyed. And Memphis' worst race riot in history. Many Black freed men and veterans of the Civil War were forced to leave their city permanently. Even city police and firefighters made of 1/3 of the rioting White mob. That laid waste to the Freedmen's neighborhoods. No one was persecuted after this Black massacre. How and why did this happen. After the capture of Memphis by Union forces in 1862.

The city became a haven for refugees' slaves, trying to escape their former slave owners. From 1860 to 1865 the Black population in Memphis increased from 3000 to nearly 20,000. However, former slave owners in Memphis resented both their labor shortages and the groups of freed Black People being in their city. And urged the U.S. military to act. The US military decided to detain many Black People. Classified them as quote unquote vagrants into custody and forced them to accept a labor contract on plantations. According to local Reverend T. Bliss in a letter to a U S general. "How is it that the Colored children in Memphis even with their spelling books in their hands are caught up by your order and taken to the same place and there insolently told that they 'had better be picking cotton.' Has it come to this that the most

BLACK MASSACRES

Common rights of these poor Black people are thus to be trampled upon for the benefit of those who have wronged them all their days?" Black soldiers attempted to intervene on behalf of their people forced back onto plantations. Tensions arose in the city. Incidents of police brutality skyrocketed. The local police arrested the Black soldiers for minor offenses and treated them more harshly than their white counterparts. They also shoved and beat Black civilians on the streets, for the crime of quote unquote insolence. Finally on May 1st, 1866. A large group of Black soldiers and their families, wives and children Included. Where hosting an impromptu Street party. A group of Memphis police officers was called to the scene. When the soldiers refused to disperse, the officers called her reinforcements. An officer accidentally shot himself in the leg while showing his gun. Blaming the injury on the Black People. The lies of this story escalated, resulting in an officer being shot and killed. City police and angry White residents began to fire at and killed several of these Black soldiers.

"Your Old Father Abe Lincoln Is Dead and Damned": Black Soldiers and the Memphis Race Riot of 1866"

Some were already fleeing or arrested. Eventually in the late evening, the White mob began destroying various Black homes in the area looting them and assaulting their residence. Some of the Black residents died when the mob forced them to stay inside their own burning houses. Schools and Churches were also targeted and burned down. The violence continued through the entire day of May 3rd. 1/3 of the White rioters were from Memphis's own Police and Fire Department who engaged in the killing and looting. Even the Raping of a few Black women. By the end of May 3rd, 46 Black People were murdered. Five Black women were Raped. 285 more were injured and over 100 homes and buildings were burned to ashes. No arrests were ever made after these riots!!! Now it says 100 homes and buildings were burnt to ashes. These buildings had to be grocery stores, clothing stores, Barber shops, clubs, etc. All of these things were burnt down. Now. I hope you understand how these Black massacres were all kind of like Black Wall Street in Tulsa, OK.

REFERENCE

"Your Old Father Abe Lincoln Is Dead and Damned": Black Soldiers and the Memphis Race Riot of 1866" Kevin R. Hardwick/ Journal of Social History Vol. 27, No. 1 (Autumn, 1993), pp. 109-128 (20 pages) Published By: Oxford University Press/https://www.jstor.org/stable/3789131/

CHAPTER THREE
THE THIRD BLACK MASSACRE.
NEW ORLEANS, LA 1866.

The New Orleans Black massacre of 1866, at the city's Mechanics' Institute; is a part of a series of episodes that happen during the Reconstruction era. Recent killings of Black People have fueled a lack of trust between communities of color and police. In 1866, a Black Massacre happened at the hands of police in downtown New Orleans. That was during Reconstruction. These episodes are the reasons why many Black people in America were and are, in fear, of the police. Back to 1866, just one year after the Civil War ended; It was a very tense time back then. Louisiana Republicans wanted to explore giving Blacks the right to vote. They called a convention to consider it in the state constitution. It seems very noble and, in many ways, but everything was politics. And people change loyalties strategically.

Republicans, arguably, supported giving Blacks the right to vote in hopes it would help their party maintain political power. Louisiana was under Union occupation during the Civil War and had a Republican governor by the end of it. But in 1866, Andrew Johnson was the President of the United States, and a big fan of Home Rule. Home Rule was letting former Confederate states make their own decisions again if they also obeyed federal laws. This concerned Republicans in the South, who felt they would lose ground under Home Rule. At such a pivotal moment, Republicans realized they needed the support of freed Black men to maintain political power.

And they got it. Black men, Women and children showed up to support the lawmakers in changing the state constitution. A procession of 70-100 Black men had proceeded to this point. They organized themselves down in the Faubourg Marigny. That stood on Canal Street, right where Burgundy turns into Roosevelt Way, to describe what happened on July 30, 1866, outside the constitutional convention. When these Freedmen, many of them Civil War veterans, showed up. They were assaulted by White attackers, they were verbally and physically assaulted, someone actually shot at them. They fired back, no one was injured. They fought off the attackers and proceeded right down here on Roosevelt Way, to what is today the Roosevelt Hotel. Back then it was the Mechanics' Institute.

This convention had been highly publicized, everyone around town knew it was happening, whether they were for or against Blacks gaining the right to vote. Bell crosses Canal Street to the entrance of what is now the famous luxury hotel. This is where the street was filled with men, women, and children, again who were excited at the thought of an interracial democracy, the hopes of an interracial government. You could say we were happy with the thoughts of being a real citizen ("An Absolute Massacre: The 1866 Riot at The Mechanics' Institute." WWNO, 14 July 2016). The parade of Black marchers had thwarted off the White mob on the other side of Canal, but once they made it to the Mechanics' Institute, where the convention was taking place inside, they were hit by more violence. A gang of White supremacists and ex-Confederates attacked. Fire sirens went off, signaling police to attack. They were sent by the Mayor John T. Monroe. There was panic because the police and firemen, armed, surrounded that building and began advancing. The attack was premeditated. Lead police chief Harry T. Hayes, at the time, was recruiting policemen from Confederate veterans. They stormed in and started shooting, chasing people down the street. When the attackers finally ran out of bullets, nearly 50 people lay dead, mostly Black. People claim there were over a hundred injured in all of this. That's very conservative though, it's thought that as many as 200, maybe more people were injured in all of this. Federal troops had also been called in, well after things got bloody, and it was obviously too late. Black People lay limp, heads bashed in with bricks, broken bodies thrown from windows, landing on top of emptied bullet casings and abandoned knives. It was an absolute massacre. And there were immediate consequences.

The Black Massacre, not a riot of 1866, as horrible as it may have been, was actually very useful to the Republican Party because it helped them get the 14th & 15th amendment passed for Black People and it gave them a concrete example of the kind of problems that the former Confederates were causing in the South. It was one of those instances where they couldn't have done anything more detrimental to their own cause. And I think in a way these returning Confederates were given enough rope, just enough to hang themselves.

The Mechanics' Institute Massacre, combined with another that happened two months earlier in Memphis, Tennessee, essentially served as a reset button for post-war policy in the South. These events were top stories in the national media and influenced voters who headed to the polls that fall. And of course, elect a radical super majority to Congress. The radical super majority enacts the Reconstruction Acts which breaks up the South into military districts. I often teach my students that if you don't have the Black Massacre of 1866, you probably don't have the Fourteenth and Fifteenth Amendments in the way that they appear." The 14th Amendment granted citizenship to former enslaved people in 1868. The Fifteenth Amendment, giving Black men the right to vote, passed in 1870. Despite the progress it helped achieve, the massacre was a tragedy. There were no convictions in the aftermath. Nobody went to jail. This reminds me of many recent, contemporary incidents of police violence against people of color. Thinking about Tamir Rice, the 12-year-old who was gunned down. That was settled, it wasn't considered a murder! And the country's waiting to see what will happen to the officers who shot and killed Philando Castile, in his car in Minnesota, with his girlfriend beside him. And the day before that, Alton Sterling in Baton Rouge.

After Mechanics' Institute Massacre, The New Orleans Tribune continued to follow the incident for months, both in news coverage and poetry. Those published poems written by Afro-Creoles that Bruce is translating. Camille Naudin was one of the most militant voices among the poets of the Tribune. He wrote a poem to commemorate the massacre called, Ode to the Martyrs. It was written for the one-year anniversary of the 1866, Black Massacre, so it was printed on the day the following year. The same day that there was a memorial ceremony at the Mechanics' Institute. 'Ode to the Martyrs' is really an elegy that enumerates a number of the victims who were killed, in pretty dramatic fashion, and celebrates their sacrifice. The poet mourns the Black victims of the White mob who were brutally massacred, while former Confederate leader Jefferson Davis remained alive, and free at the time. There was a perception among Unionists that he was getting off Scott free.

A former Black Union soldier Victor Lacroix, who is from a really well-known New Orleans family, who was pretty much torn to shreds by the White Confederate mob. Was remembered in a translated poem. At the end he writes "But for Mulattos, Blacks and Whites, this fact I must tell: Victor Lacroix is dead. Jeff Davis lives still.'"

The New Orleans massacre 1866, also known as, An Absolute Massacre: The 1866 Riot at The Mechanics' Institute. Happened one year after the Civil War had ended. Republicans in the state of Louisiana were looking to give newly freed Black Men the right to vote. They went so far as to call the convention, trying to get it enshrined in the state constitution. The main reason for this was that the White voters, many of them Democratic Confederate veterans. Were continually passing racist laws. Laws which would substantially reduce the Black Citizens of that state to a status that was just like slavery none the less. The White mob began attacking the Black

11

marchers' Lucy and John Pierre Kaplan. A witness to the violence later recalled, I saw the people fall like flies. Kaplan and his son were both brutally attacked, suffering devastating wounds. The federal troops finally showed up. More than 40 Black Men were dead, with over 100 wounded from the fighting. The Black Massacre took place outside the Mechanics' Institute in New Orleans. As Black and White delegates attended the convention, which was called the Louisiana Constitutional Convention. The conventional reason being because Louisiana State legislature had recently passed the Black Codes and refused to extend voting rights to Black Men. Also, on May 12, 1866, four years of Union Army impose Martial Law ended. And Mayor John T. Monroe, who had headed city government before the Civil War was reinstated in acting man. Monroe had been an active supporter of the Confederacy and delegation of 130 Black New Orleans residents. They marched behind the US flag toward the Mechanics Institute on Roosevelt Way. Organized and led by a mob of ex Confederates White supremacists and members of the New Orleans Police force, to the institute to block their way. The mayor claimed they intended to put down any unrest that may come from the convention. But the real reason was to prevent the delegates from meeting. The delegation came to within a couple of blocks of the institute and shots were fired. The group was allowed to proceed to the meeting hall once they reached the institute. The police and a White mob members attacked the Black People, beating some of the marchers, while others rushed inside the building for safety. The police and White mob surrounded the institute and opened fire on the building. Shooting indiscriminately into the windows. Then the White mob rushed into the building and began to fire into the crowd of delegates. When the White mob ran out of ammunition, they were beaten back by the Black people still inside the building. The White mob left the building regrouped and return. Breaking down the door and again firing on the mostly unarmed delegates. As the firing continued, some delegates attempted to flee or surrender. Some of those who surrendered, primarily Blacks, were killed on the spot. Those who ran would be chased. As the killing spread over several blocks around the institute. By this point both the rioters and victims, included people who were never at the institute Black People. were shot on the street or pulled off of street cars to be beaten or killed. By the end of the massacre. At least 200 Black Union War Veterans were killed, including 40 delegates. At the convention, altogether 238 people were killed, 46 others were wounded.

Family as we take this journey together. Hopefully, you will learn as I did, this sets a dangerous precedence. Because these acts have been happening since the very origins of this country. The racists hate us and you most likely will not change their minds. Some White people may get offended by my words, but the truth should set you free. And I am not writing this for them. They could have been writing these books. And because of them not doing so. It allows their children to live life like none of this happened or it doesn't matter. Well, it does!! And I will continue to teach what I know to help people grow. Maham the Mentor.

REFERENCE

"An Absolute Massacre: The 1866 Riot At The Mechanics' Institute." WWNO, 14 July 2016, https://www.wwno.org/podcast/tripod-new-orleans-at-300/2016-07-14/an-absolute-massacre-the-1866-riot-at-the-mechanics-institute.

CHAPTER FOUR
THE FOURTH BLACK MASSACRE.
CAMILLA, GA 1868.

The "Camilla Black Massacre took place in Camilla, Georgia, on Saturday, September 19, 1868"(Sept. 19, 1868: Camilla Massacre | Zinn Education Project." Zinn Education Project, 30 May 2021). It followed the expulsion of the Original 33 Black members of the Georgia General Assembly earlier that month. Among those expelled was southwest Georgia representative Philip Joiner. On September 19, Joiner led a twenty-five-mile march of several hundred Blacks (Freedmen), and a few Whites, from Albany, Georgia, to Camilla, the Mitchell County seat, to attend a Republican political rally on the courthouse square. Estimates of the number of participants range from 150 to 300.

The local sheriff and "citizens committee" in the majority-White town warned the Black and White activists that they would be met with violence, and demanded that they surrender their guns, even though carrying weapons was legal and customary at the time. The marchers refused to give up their guns and continued to the courthouse square, where a group of local Whites, quickly deputized by the sheriff, fired upon them. This assault forced the Republicans and Black Freedmen to retreat into the swamps as locals gave chase, killing an estimated nine to fifteen of the Black rally participants while wounding forty others. Whites proceeded through the countryside over the next two weeks, beating and warning Black men that they would be killed if they tried to vote in the coming election. The Camilla Black Massacre was the culmination of smaller acts of anti-Black violence committed by White inhabitants that had plagued southwest Georgia since the end of the Civil War.

The Black Massacre received national publicity, prompted Congress to return Georgia to military occupation, and was a factor in the 1868 U.S.

presidential election.

The Camilla Black Massacre remained part of southwest Georgia's hidden past until 1998, when Camilla residents publicly acknowledged the Black Massacre for the first time and commemorated its victims.

REFERENCE

"Sept. 19, 1868: Camilla Massacre | Zinn Education Project." Zinn Education Project, 30 May 2021, https://www.zinnedproject.org/news/tdih/camilla-massacre/..

CHAPTER 5
THE FIFTH BLACK MASSACRE.
OPELOUSAS, LA 1868.

The Opelousas Black Massacre occurred on "September 28, 1868, in Opelousas, St. Landry Parish, Louisiana, United States" (Matthew Christensen. (2012, May 1). Beginning with the execution of 27 Black prisoners, Whites conducted widespread attacks on former enslaved Black People in the vicinity and are believed to have killed in total up to 200-250 of them from September 28 until November 3.

At the time, Whites referred to events as the Opelousas Riot, as if caused by an outbreak of violence by Blacks, and a minority of historians continue to refer to it by this name. The Real name of this event is The Black Massacre by evil White People of Opelousas, Louisiana. They are not riots of Black People in America in the 1800s. They had no power to participate in a riot. These events were Massacres. If you catch a person calling any of these events a riot, please correct them immediately.

To the elections in the fall of 1868, some formerly enslaved Blacks from Opelousas attempted to join a Democratic Party-political group organized in the neighboring, larger town of Washington. Whites rejected them, and Democrats in Opelousas, mainly members of the Seymour Knights, the local unit of the white organization Knights of the White Camellia, visited Washington to violently drive the Blacks out of the party.

In response, Emerson Bentley, an 18-year-old Ohio-born White school teacher and editor of The Landry Progress, a Republican newspaper in Opelousas, wrote an article that described the attack by the Seymour Knights against the Black Democrats. He suggested that such events should persuade Blacks to remain loyal to the Republican Party. Bentley was known as an advocate of education for the children of Black freedmen and of Creole people (who had been free before the war). He also helped adult men of both

16

groups to register to vote. Shortly after the article appeared, Bentley was assaulted at his class by three White men and severely beaten. Afterward, Bentley quickly fled town and ran for his life to reach the North.

Due to Bentley's sudden disappearance, reports circulated that the teacher had been killed because of his article. Several local armed formerly enslaved Black People banded together to retaliate and marched toward the county seat of Opelousas. Some left the march when they learned that Bentley had not been murdered. The armed Blacks were met by armed Whites determined to defend their town, many of whom had been rallied by The Knights of the White Camellia. Due to local laws restricting gun ownership by Blacks, the White Democrats had the overwhelming advantage in weapons, as well as in numbers. Shooting broke out on both sides, and the Whites captured twenty-nine Black prisoners. On September 29, all the captured prisoners, with the exception of two men, were taken from the prison and killed by over thirty armed Democrats. The dead included twelve Black Republican leaders.

After that, Whites continued attacks on Blacks in St. Landry Parish for weeks, killing them on the street or country roads. Historians have disputed the total death toll of the Black Massacre, and accounts at the time were a subject of controversy. Three White Republicans and two Democrats were killed in the initial assault in Opelousas. Republicans said that around 200-300 Blacks were killed in total by White insurgents (White historians try to use words like, White insurgents, as a weak way to brush over the evilness white people did, just call them White people, no insurgents!!), but the Democrats said this claim was fraudulent and approximately 25-30 Blacks were killed. Carolyn E. DeLatte writing in 1976 describes the discrepancy between Republican and Democrat numbers but points out a report by a "highly partisan" Democrat paper that didn't support their claims, with reported 100 killed Blacks and perhaps 100 more wounded. Matthew Christensen pinpoints that paper as Franklin Planter's Banner, edited by Daniel Dennett who had helped form the Knights in Louisiana. It was also reported that 30-50 Whites were killed. Many historians of the early 21st century have concluded that the Republicans' estimate was more accurate, given the death toll in similar events. Jesse M. Lee, a lieutenant for United States Army, was sent by Freedmen's Bureau to investigate the turmoil in the state and estimated 223 total deaths had occurred in St. Landry Parish during the massacre, but he also had to rely on Democratic press as it was impossible to procure full evidence in the state of lawlessness and intimidation. The Board of Registrars for St. Landry Parish estimated over 200 total deaths. Matthew Christensen finds in 2012 that the total number of dead probably fell between 200-250 Black people from September 28 until November 3.

BLACK MASSACRES

The post-Civil-war period was one of widespread violence in the South, as Whites struggled to assert their dominance over the freedmen and to regain their political power. A majority of the newly freed Black People strongly supported the Republican Party, which had achieved their emancipation; this angered southern Democrats, who did not want to give up any political power, especially to the party that had defeated them at war. The war was considered to continue, But by White insurgents like Historian says? These were just poor uneducated White People, who worked for White supremacy and killed hundreds if not thousands of Black People and their sympathizers before the end of Reconstruction. The Ku Klux Klan (KKK) rapidly developed chapters across the South, but such groups as the Knights of the White Camellia, the Red Shirts, and White rifle clubs were also active gangs that existed back then. Such White racist gangs sought to suppress Blacks and those who supported them through various scare tactics, physical violence, and even murder.

REFERENCE

Matthew Christensen. (2012, May 1). The 1868 st. landry massacre: Reconstruction's deadliest episode of violence. UWM Digital Commons. https://dc.uwm.edu/etd/190/

CHAPTER 6
THE SIXTH BLACK MASSACRE.
ST. BERNARD PARISH, LA 1868.

"The Bernard Parish Black Massacre was on a chilly Louisiana afternoon in October 1868, Louis Wilson left the courthouse, where he'd testified in an ongoing case. A Black man named Wilson was a freedman living in St. Bernard Parish, a rural community outside the city of New Orleans. The Civil War had been over for three years, and the 14th Amendment, which gave Wilson full citizenship, had passed just three months before" (Author: Patrick Young. (2020, February 22). Across the South, tensions were high because of the upcoming presidential election that would decide the fate of Reconstruction.

Wilson rode home alongside the winding Mississippi River, where he was confronted by a group of armed White men on horseback. He was aware that freed Black people had been killed the day before, but wrongly assumed that the carnage had ended. The men ordered him to dismount, and one of them struck his jaw with the butt of a shotgun. Wilson was thrown into a wagon with other captive Black freedmen and transported to a makeshift prison.

Later that evening, Wilson and a few others were dragged out of their cells, lined up, and blasted with shotguns. Everyone was killed except Wilson, who somehow crawled into a nearby cane field and waited for three days until he felt safe. Over the next few days, White men tore through the parish, attempting to eliminate any further threats, leaving behind them a trail of Black corpses. Estimates of the massacre range from 35 to more than 100 murdered.

Historically, this event has usually been labeled "the St. Bernard riots." It should be termed the 1868 St. Bernard Parish Black Massacre—one of the most brutal episodes of racist violence in U.S. history, as well as one of the most forgotten. I first came across it while I was in prison reading

19

encyclopedias. What I discovered was that a murderous rampage had occurred in my parents' home State, and almost no one knew. The perpetrators never discussed their atrocities. Local records were lost due to numerous floods, including Hurricane Katrina in 2005. I have tried to research these events for years, driving to and from Louisiana, down roads and past former cane fields that were once the bloody battleground of Reconstruction. As I delved deeper into U.S. Congressional archives, I uncovered investigations commissioned by the Freedmen's Bureau and the Louisiana State Legislature, and correspondence with then-President Andrew Johnson. But my most startling discovery was that several of my family members were the descendants of those involved, victims and perpetrators alike. The racial tension that sparked the Black massacre was not unique to St. Bernard Parish. By 1868, the South had lost the Civil War and was struggling to rebuild its battered economy, which had depended heavily on an enslaved population. Louisiana was under federal military occupation during Reconstruction, and Black males had obtained the right to vote.

The stakes were high for Southern elites in the presidential election, the first since the end of the war. If they could solidify a win for Horatio Seymour, a "Copperhead" Democrat who had promised to roll back Reconstruction policies, they might regain some of the power they had lost. Seymour railed against "Negro supremacy" and proudly painted himself as the "White Man's" candidate. Whites believed that a victory by Seymour's Republican opponent, Ulysses S. Grant, former commander of the Union Army, would pave the way for racial equality, leading to the collapse of economic and political systems that favored Whites in the South. After the Civil War ended, many impoverished Whites faced increased economic hardship. Wealthier Whites exploited their fears and blamed freed Blacks as the cause of their ills. Newspapers owned by these elites were full of anti-Republican and racialized propaganda. Many poor Whites perceived Reconstruction as a form of government occupation that disadvantaged them while favoring freed Black people. Conditions were ripe for dangerous rhetoric to turn lethal.

Violence in St. Bernard Parish started a pre-election pro-Seymour rally on Sunday, October 25, 1868. As White marchers passed by Eugene Lock, a freed Black man, they yelled for him to "hurrah" for Seymour. Lock refused. Someone grabbed Lock to intimidate him into submission, but as Lock remained steadfast, the crowd grew increasingly agitated. One White man tried to stab Lock with a knife, while another shot at him, narrowly missing his target. Lock drew his own pistol and fired back, hitting the shoulder of the man who had fired at him. Outnumbered, Lock tried to escape, but was shot in the head and mortally wounded before finally being stabbed. As news of the altercation sped through the small community, men grabbed their arms and prepared for battle.

Yet there was no battle, only a one-sided rampage by marauding Whites. Throughout the week, armed White militias hunted freed Black people like Louis Wilson, as if for sport. In his testimony to an agent of the Freedmen's Bureau shortly after the tragedy, Wilson said of the parish that he once called home: "This is such a cold place, I am afraid I will die here."

According to an 1868 report by the Freedmen's Bureau and an 1869 report by the Louisiana General Assembly, White mobs broke into homes and shot residents at close range, conducted executions in the streets, and killed those who tried to intervene. They plundered former slave quarters and stole items they found useful, most notably registration papers. A Black pregnant woman was hacked to death by White men with bowie-knives next to the courthouse. A White police officer was murdered by the White mobs for trying to keep the peace. It was 19th-century terrorism.

And it succeeded. While countless numbers of freed Black people fell victim to the violence of White people, one White Boy, Pablo San Feliu, was killed by freed Blacks in retaliation. Any legitimate supervisor of the presidential election was jailed, executed, or fled. Grant received only one vote in St. Bernard Parish as Seymour swept the state. According to historian John C. Rodrigue, "Republicans captured the presidency in 1868, but White terror carried the day in Louisiana."

Despite the federal investigation, no one was arrested for the killing of the freed Black people. Black survivors identified White neighbors as their assailants, but no justice was sought. Instead, more than 100 freed Black people were arrested by local authorities and vigilantes for the killing of Pablo San Feliu. Over time, the Black Massacre faded into obscurity. To this day, its only physical reminder is the tombstone of Pablo San Feliu, located in St. Bernard Cemetery, which reads:

Pablo San Feliu
Assassinated by Slaves To
Incited by Carpetbag Rule
Died Oct. 1869

The inaccuracies on San Feliu's tombstone misrepresent the circumstances surrounding his death. The incorrect date suggests that it was erected a significant amount of time after the Black Massacre, perhaps memorializing his death as if he were a martyr. The engraver referred to the freed Black people as "slaves." Most importantly, by placing blame on carpetbaggers, the derogatory term applied to Northerners and other outsiders who had migrated to the South during Reconstruction, the inscription implies that San Feliu was an innocent murder victim. But he was just a guilty criminal and a weak, cowardly, evil, white punk.

Nearly a decade after the Black Massacre, Reconstruction officially ended. By 1877 Louisiana had returned to "home rule," which meant that the Black population was no longer protected by Federal occupation. The new state government focused on suppression of Black voters. The new state constitution allowed for arbitrary literacy tests and issued poll taxes, while also granting grandfather clauses that allowed White people to circumvent these obstacles to voting. By 1898, the Black voting bloc had declined from 164,000 to a mere 1,342. By 1910, that number dropped to 730, less than a half-percent of eligible Black men. Their political voice was silenced throughout Louisiana.

A Black massacre of this magnitude deserves a place in history. I incorporated the story of the St. Bernard Parish Massacre into my teaching curriculum for young men. So, they could be made aware of their country's history and its relevance today. Seeing how easily Trump got people to follow him, even some Black people, we can now examine how dangerous rhetoric can lead to deadly actions and the dire consequences of racist scapegoating.

My students are often shocked when they learn about this chapter of their country's history. But it provides opportunities to have open dialogue with one another about our roots, and to bring these conversations into our own homes. I am sometimes criticized by White people in the community for unearthing buried history. Some have claimed that the timing was inappropriate, that it would worsen existing racial tensions. However, most people in the community have been supportive and eager to know more. The progress that has brought people closer together in the community can only be honored through a deeper understanding of history. These relationships epitomize how far race relations in Louisiana have advanced due to people pushing against barriers, from that lone man who voted for Grant in St. Bernard Parish to those who waged the nation's first major bus boycott in Baton Rouge nearly a century later.

However, the reversal of many gains made by Black Louisianans after Reconstruction reminds us that these advances are not inherently linear or permanent. The continuing problems of mass incarceration, police brutality, and educational inequity underscore the effects of the disenfranchisement of huge swaths of the Black population. Understanding complex historical events like the St. Bernard Parish Black Massacre shows how we can continue to bridge racial divides today. Communities should not hide from such history but embrace it.

REFERENCE

Author: Patrick Young. (2020, February 22). St. bernard parish massacre of blacks in louisiana october 25-26, 1868 - the reconstruction era. The Reconstruction Era. https://thereconstructionera.com/st-bernard-parish-massacre-of-blacks-in-louisiana-october-25-26-1868/

CHAPTER 7
THE SEVENTH BLACK MASSACRE.
COLFAX, LA 1873.

The Colfax Black Massacre occurred on April 13, 1873. "The battle-turned-massacre took place in the small town of Colfax, Louisiana as a clash between Blacks and Whites. Three Whites and an estimated 150 Blacks died in the fight" (Michael Stolp-Smith. (2019, October 3).

The Black Massacre took place against the backdrop of racial tensions following the hotly contested Louisiana governor's race of 1872. While the Republicans narrowly won the contest and retained control of the state, White Democrats, angry over the defeat, vowed revenge. In Colfax Parish (county) as in other areas of the state, they organized a White militia to directly challenge the mostly Black state militia under the control of the governor.

Colfax Parish reflected the political and racial divide in Louisiana. Its 4,600 voters in the 1872 election were split between approximately 2,400 hundred mostly Black Republican voters and 2,200 White Democratic voters. One incident however, touched off the Colfax Black Massacre. On March 28, local White Democratic leaders called for armed supporters to help them take the Colfax Parish Courthouse from the Black and White GOP officeholders on April 1. The Republicans responded by urging their mostly Black supporters to defend them. Although nothing happened on April 1, the next day fighting erupted between the two groups.

On April 13, Easter Sunday, more than 300 armed white men, including members of White supremacist organizations such as the Knights of White Camellia and the Ku Klux Klan, attacked the Courthouse building. When the militia maneuvered a cannon to fire on the Courthouse, some of the sixty Black defenders fled while others surrendered. When the leader of the attackers, James Hadnot, was accidentally shot by one of his own men, the

White militia responded by shooting the Black prisoners. Those who were wounded in the earlier battle, particularly Black militia members, were singled out for execution. The indiscriminate killing spread to Black People who had not been at the courthouse and continued into the night.

All told, approximately 150 Black People were killed, including 48 who were murdered after the battle. Only three Whites were killed, and few were injured in the largely one-sided battle of Colfax.

On April 14, the state militia under the control of Republican Governor William Kellogg arrived at the scene and recorded the carnage. New Orleans police and federal troops also arrived in the next few days to reestablish order. A total of 97 White militia men were arrested and charged with violation of the U.S. Enforcement Act of 1870 (also known as the Ku Klux Klan Act). A handful of them were convicted but were eventually released in 1875 when the U.S. Supreme Court in United States v. Cruikshank ruled the Enforcement Act was unconstitutional. No one was ever arrested by the state of Louisiana or by intimidated local officials

.

REFERENCE

Michael Stolp-Smith. (2019, October 3). The colfax massacre (1873) •. BlackPast Is Dedicated to Providing a Global Audience with Reliable and Accurate Information on the History of African America and of People of African Ancestry around the World. We Aim to Promote Greater Understanding through This Knowledge to Generate Constructive Change in Our Society. https://www.blackpast.org/african-american-history/colfax-massacre-1873/

.

CHAPTER 8
THE EIGHTH BLACK MASSACRE.
EUFAULA, ALABAMA 1873.

This Black Massacre happened on November 3, 1874, in Eufaula, Alabama. Our history books call this horrific event The Election Massacre of 1874, or Coup of 1874. "During the Civil War, Eufaula, Alabama, was at once a Confederate stronghold, the commercial center of Barbour County, and home to more Black people than white. After Emancipation, ratification of the Fifteenth Amendment guaranteed voting rights for Black men. This empowered Barbour County's new Black electorate to end white supremacist officials' control over the county" (Eufaula, alabama. (2020, June 11). In 1870, Black voters helped elect Elias Keils, a white candidate who supported the aims of Reconstruction, to the position of City Court Judge. Four years later, when Keils ran for re-election, local white residents determined to regain political dominance in the county used terror and intimidation to suppress Black votes, ultimately waging a deadly Black Massacre that left dozens of Black people dead.

As the 1874 election neared, white employers openly fired any Black workers who intended to vote for Keils. False rumors spread that Black resident planned to violently drive white voters from the polls, and white residents began stockpiling guns near Eufaula polling sites. Seeing the threat of election day violence, Keils tried to notify state and federal officials of the danger, but Alabama's Attorney General rebuffed the warning and A.S. Daggett, captain of federal troops stationed in Eufaula, claimed it would violate his orders to use federal soldiers to protect Black voters.

Despite the risk, hundreds of Black People marched to the downtown Eufaula polling site on November 3. Some were immediately arrested and jailed on fraud accusations. Around noon, several white men forced a Black man into an alley and threatened to arrest him if he did not vote against civil

26

rights. Black witnesses protested and a pistol was fired—white people claimed a Black man had fired a shot at them while many Black people insisted a white man had fired a shot into the air. Soon afterward, a large mob of white men retrieved stockpiled guns stored nearby, gathered in the street and in the upstairs windows of surrounding buildings, and fired "indiscriminately" into the crowd of mostly unarmed Black voters.

A historical marker in Barbour County, Alabama, erected in 1979, describes the 1874 Eufaula Black Massacre as a "riot." Every time that we notice, or we see historians label these Black Massacres as a simple "massacre" or a "riot", it is a lame attempt to brush over and belittle the magnitude of the situation done by White people. Very disrespectful to Black people.

Within minutes, 400 shots had been fired, leaving at least six Black people dead and injuring as many as 80 people. Many survivors fled, including an estimated 500 Black people who had not yet voted. One Black man who survived later recalled that, when the shooting stopped, he heard the white crowd cheer, "Hurrah for the white man's party." Later that day, a white mob attacked another county polling station in Spring Hill, Alabama, where Keils was the election supervisor. The White mob destroyed the ballot box, burned the ballots inside, and killed Keils's teenage son.

Newspapers described the violence as a "riot," but a Congressional representative later characterized the attack as a Black massacre. Sentiments published in the local white press praised the attack: "Big riot today. Several killed and many other hurt—some badly—but none of our friends among them. The white man's goose hangs high. Three cheers from Eufaula." Although the identities of many white perpetrators of the Black massacre were known, no white person was ever convicted. Instead, a Black man named Hilliard Miles was convicted and imprisoned for perjury after identifying members of the white mob. Decades later, Braxton Bragg Comer, whom Mr. Miles had named as a perpetrator of the Black Massacre, was elected governor of Alabama.

The Eufaula Black Massacre and its aftermath showed Black residents that exercising their new legal rights—particularly by voting—made them targets for deadly attacks and they could not depend on authorities for protection. The result was mass voter suppression. While 1,200 Black Eufaula residents voted in the 1874 election, only 10 cast ballots in 1876. That legacy remains. Today, the population of Barbour County is nearly 50 percent Black, but white officials hold 8 of 12 elected county positions. In 2016, the county had the highest voter purge rate in the United States.

During Reconstruction, Black voters lost their lives in Eufaula and many more were disenfranchised because they supported pro-Reconstruction

BLACK MASSACRES

Republican candidates who pushed for Black citizenship rights at a time when white supremacy dominated the Southern Democratic party. This division would continue until major party realignments during the 20th century civil rights movement. Today, public memory of Reconstruction violence in Barbour County is reduced to one historical marker erected in 1979, which describes the "Election Riot of 1874" as a "bloody episode that marked the end of Republican domination in Barbour County." In downtown Eufaula, the streets where Black voters were shot down for voting more than 140 years ago now host a towering Confederate monument erected by the United Daughters of the Confederacy in 1904. S.H. Dent, a former Confederate soldier who witnessed and possibly helped commit the Black Massacre, spoke at the monument's unveiling.

REFERENCE

Eufaula, alabama. (2020, June 11). EJI Reports. https://eji.org/report/reconstruction-in-america/a-truth-that-needs-telling/sidebar/eufaula-alabama/

CHAPTER 9
THE 9TH BLACK MASSACRE.
VICKSBURG, MISSISSIPPI 1874.

The "Vicksburg Black Massacre occurred on Dec. 7, 1874, in Mississippi, with estimates ranging from 75 to 300 Black People were killed. Whites attacked Black citizens who had organized to defend Peter Crosby. Formerly enslaved and a veteran of the Union army, Crosby had been forced to resign from his elected role as sheriff" (Dec. 7, 1874: Vicksburg massacre | zinn education project. (2021, May 30).

During reconstruction, racist groups were being created all over the South. Ones like the White League of the White-Line movement more generally, in Louisiana and Mississippi. They committed to drawing the racial line in politics and inviting all white men without regard to former party affiliations to unite, the racist White league was first organized in Opelousas, Louisiana in late April of 1874 and then spread very rapidly.

They built their foundation off the principles established by the Klan, another racist group created just to stop Black people from becoming successful. The Knights of the White Camelia — a Union army commander regarded the league as a "Second edition of the White Camilla campaign of 1868" (A.K.A. The Fourth Black Massacre, Camilla Massacre) — but was even more directly aligned with the Democratic party. Indeed, leagues were often little more than local Democratic clubs converted into paramilitary companies. "If the democratic party is arrayed against the negro and the republicans," the Opelousas Courier proclaimed, "it becomes a White League, and no one can object to its efficient organization."

Racist White Leaguers surely recognized that the federal government was losing interest in interfering in southern politics and sustaining Republican regimes by military means. But they also responded to the growing assertiveness of Black People within the Republican party, which showed itself in the rising incidence of Black office holding.

By this time the White-Line counterparts in Vicksburg, Mississippi, had demonstrated how paramilitary mobilization and very definite intimidation could bring electoral success even where Black voters held decided numerical sway.

If anything, still held back a full-scale white paramilitary offensive, it was removed when, in the November elections of 1874, congressional Democrats won control of the House of Representatives for the first time since southern slaveholders had rebelled against the national government. In Vicksburg, White-Liners seemed to commemorate the event by moving quickly to complete the work they had begun in the summer. This time, they focused on the county, rather than the municipal, government, which was almost wholly dominated by Black Republicans, including the sheriff Peter Crosby, a Native Mississippian who had served in the Union army during the war. Meeting in early December, they demanded the resignations of all the Black officials and pressured Crosby to yield under what he regarded as a threat of assassination. Crosby then headed to the state capital for help.

Governor and Gen. Adelbert C. Ames was a Republican. The party's radical faction turned a sympathetic ear. He ordered the White riotous and disorderly persons who had expelled from office the legally elected sheriff to disperse and retire peaceably and submit to the legally constituted authorities. He also instructed an All-White Warren County militia company to cooperate with Crosby's effort to regain office and suppress the white mob and suggested that Crosby should summon a posse for further assistance.

Ame's orders did little to change the behavior or temper of the Vicksburg whites, but Crosby's call for a posse revealed a strong foundation of loyalty and organizational readiness among Black People in the surrounding countryside. With dispatch, owing to the churches, political clubs, and other institutions of Black community life, a major mobilization took place. As several hundred Blacks marched in three columns toward Vicksburg, even Crosby feared the consequences and tried to turn some of them back. It was too late. White people opened fire, and despite some brief standoffs, the Blacks were forced to flee. For another ten days, some of the young white participants, joined by reinforcements from across the river in Louisiana, stayed on the war path.

When the smoke cleared, at least twenty-nine Black People had been killed and a great many more had been wounded and terrorized. The seat of county government remained in the hands of the racist White-Liners. And Peter Crosby, briefly held prisoner, was compelled to resign yet again.

Ames called the state legislature into special session and together they succeeded in convincing Grant to send a company of federal troops to quell the disturbances in Vicksburg and reinstall Crosby as sheriff. But Crosby's days in office were numbered and so too, it appeared, were those of

Republicans over much of the state. For the several-month White-Line campaign in Vicksburg and Warren County amounted to a rehearsal for redemption in Mississippi.

Torchlight processions, paramilitary drilling, the disruption of Republican political meetings, the harassment of Black workers, the intimidation and assassination of Black leaders, the driving off of local officeholders, and the disabling of armed Black resistance — all of which made their appearance in Vicksburg in 1874 — were to come into concerted use in 1875 in counties that previously had safe Republican majorities. This was the 9th Black Massacre that happened in the U.S. after the Civil War. Many of the Black Massacres, such as this one, were designed to reassert White supremacy during Reconstruction. And they were able to do most of this because of voting and having us be intimidated or scared to vote. That's why it amazes me to see so many Black people in today's time, talking about our vote doesn't count or don't vote. Our vote does count and has always counted. If it didn't these Black Massacres would not have happened. Now, believe that jack.

REFERENCE

Dec. 7, 1874: Vicksburg massacre | zinn education project. (2021, May 30). Zinn Education Project. https://www.zinnedproject.org/news/tdih/vicksburg-massacre/

CHAPTER 10
THE 10TH BLACK MASSACRE.
CLINTON, MISSISSIPPI 1875.

The Clinton Black Massacre began on September 4, 1875, in the small town of Clinton, Mississippi at a Republican rally to introduce the party's "candidates who were running for political office in the upcoming November elections. The immediate death toll included five Blacks and three white men. Over the next several days, an estimated fifty Blacks were killed in the massacre that followed" (Sheren Sanders. (2020, February 7).

Over 1,500 Black Republicans and their families gathered on the grounds of the former Moss Hill plantation for a barbecue and political rally. Approximately 100 whites also attended, including a few Democrats from the nearby town of Raymond. In an effort to keep the political rally peaceful, alcoholic beverages and weapons were banned, and both a Democratic and Republican candidate were invited to speak.

Judge Amos R. Johnston, the white Democratic state senate candidate, gave the opening speech with no problems from the predominantly black crowd. However, the Republican speaker and editor of the Jackson Times, Captain H.T. Fisher, was interrupted during his speech when a white Democrat in the audience called him a liar. Shortly afterwards, shots were fired, and the crowd frantically ran in all directions to get away from the danger. When the gunfire ended, a total of five Blacks, including two children, and three whites were dead, and nearly thirty others were wounded. It was reported that a white man fired the first shot, but other rumors contended that armed Black Republicans started the riot.

Later that night, a white militia associated with the Mississippi Democratic party were called in from Jackson, Vicksburg, and the surrounding areas for assistance against armed Blacks. The militia group, who called themselves Modoc after an Indian tribe in California, began a manhunt for Black People in Clinton. The following days were marked by violence and bloodshed as the white mob indiscriminately shot and killed nearly fifty Black People in Clinton and the surrounding area.

Many Blacks fled to Jackson seeking the protection of Republican governor Adelbert Ames, while others hid out in the woods to escape the terror. Although Governor Ames requested federal troops to assist in restoring order, President Ulysses Grant denied the request on September 14 and adopted a policy of non-intervention, leaving Ames and the local Black and white Republicans without protection.

The Clinton Black Massacre, and other Black Massacres, were part of white Democrats' efforts to regain political power in the November 1875 election at the end of Reconstruction in Mississippi.

REFERENCE

Sheren Sanders. (2020, February 7). The clinton, mississippi riot (1875) •. BlackPast Is Dedicated to Providing a Global Audience with Reliable and Accurate Information on the History of African America and of People of African Ancestry around the World. We Aim to Promote Greater Understanding through This Knowledge to Generate Constructive Change in Our Society. https://www.blackpast.org/african-american-history/clinton-mississippi-riot-1875/

CHAPTER 11
THE 11TH BLACK MASSACRE.
THIBODAUX, LA 1887.

"November 23, 1887, recorded the Thibodaux Black Massacre which took place in Thibodaux, Louisiana. It all began when Black sugar cane workers determined to unionize for a living wage. The group had chosen to combine their little power during the crucial harvest season. Their action was considered provocative; and it ended up sparking a disagreement that resulted in the Thibodaux Black Massacre" (SANUSI AHMODU SALIHU. (2020, March 31).

The Black sugar cane workers protested the tough working conditions, long hours, starvation of wages with echoes of the bondage their ancestors had experienced during slavery times. They were paid as little as 42 cents a day with scrip which could only be used in plantation stores. To get things even worst, they were fed subsistence meals. Their frustration grew daily with their minds gradually ready to strike.

The Black sugar cane workers received some encouragement from one of the few labor unions to organize Blacks "The Knights of Labor" to demand better treatment and $1.25 a day in cash. After several attempts by the Knights to organize the Black workers in 1874, 1880, and again in 1883 had been unsuccessful, they thought the results might be different in 1887.

The Knight urged them to wait until the rolling season was almost ongoing to suggest making a stand. As the rolling season arrived there was a thin window of time to harvest the sugar cane. Planters were unable to attract enough white strikebreakers from out of the area because of the low pay they offered.

Having this plan in mind, a White 29-year-old schoolteacher and then president of the Terrebonne chapter of the Knights of Labor, Junius Bailey, approached the White sugar cane growers with the Black cutter's demands. Now upset that Black workers were demanding an end to their paternalistic work regime. The White growers then refused to negotiate, firing the members of the Union on November 22. Strike by the Black cutters began for the next three weeks with an estimated 10,000 workers affected. Orchestrated by Hamp Keys, a Black Man and former Terrebonne Parish legislator, called a strike. Keys led a march from Houma to Southdown Plantation in Terrebonne, rallying the Black workers with a fiery speech. The sight of Black protesters riled growers, and acting with their interests in mind, the parish's Black sheriff formed a posse of whites to face down strikers. Surprised at the opposition, Key's marchers retreated. The number remains the highest to incorporate in such action in the farming industry. The strike consequently affected four different parishes including St. Mary, Lafourche, Assumption, and Terrebonne.

On November 23, as morning broke, shots started ringing out from a cornfield and two white guards got injured. From that moment the Black Massacre began. Governor Samuel D. McEnery, Democrat, and former sugar cane planter got persuaded by the sugar planters to release several units of the all-white state militia. The militia as commanded by ex-Confederate General P.G.T. Beauregard, brought a .45 caliber Gatling gun while all white paramilitary groups set up outside of the Thibodaux courthouse to form the first phase of defense. Both groups went door to door shooting any suspected Black strikers unlucky enough to cross their path.

The November 23 killing left approximately 60 Black people dead with bodies of many of the strikers dumped in unmarked graves. Those who luckily survived hid in swamps and woods and the Black Massacre continued spreading. However, the white troops got Thibodaux locked, going door after door to attempting to identify strikers. Movements were restricted for Black people from traveling in and out of the city with a pass. In 1874, nine years after slavery ended in the United States, cane cutters demanded a second emancipation. They wanted a living wage, or at least the chance to rent on shares. Planters wanted to cut wages after the lean harvest of 1873-74 coincided with an economic recession, and while Louisiana growers produced 95 percent of the nation's domestic sugar and molasses, they were losing market share to cheaper foreign sugars.

Sensing they were in a strong bargaining position, workers banded together in several sugar parishes, including St. Mary, Iberia, Terrebonne, and Lafourche, demanding cash wages of $1.25 per day, or $1.00 if meals were included.

Thibodaux Black Massacre was one of the deadliest episodes in United States labor history. The Black massacre also marked an end of any attempt for Black Farmers to unionize again until the 1930s. Statues were erected, and public areas named after many involved in the unlawful killings. Workers including women and children went anonymous, their murders marked only by their loved ones. Sugar planter Andrew Price, who participated in the attacks won a seat in Congress in 1888. And that is where I will end this.

REFERENCE

SANUSI AHMODU SALIHU. (2020, March 31). In 1887, the white militia massacred scores of black farmers in thibodaux, usa | 54history. 54History. https://54history.com/in-1887-the-white-militia-massacred-scores-of-black-farmers-in-thibodaux-usa/

CHAPTER 12
THE 12TH BLACK MASSACRE.
WILMINGTON, NC. 1898.

The Wilmington Black Massacre happened "on November 10, 1898, in Wilmington, North Carolina. Please understand that this Black Massacre was different from all the other Black Massacres because this one was a Coup d'état. The definition of a Coup d'état also known as Coup: a sudden decisive exercise of force in especially the violent overthrow or alteration of an existing government by a small group" (Adrienne LaFrance, Vann R. Newkirk II. (2021, May 16). This Black Massacre was a planned attack by a group of racist Ex-Confederate-Democrat white men who wanted to overthrow the multi-racial Republican government in Wilmington NC. the fire was the beginning of an assault that took place seven blocks east of the Cape Fear River, about 10 miles inland from the Atlantic Ocean. By sundown, Manly's newspaper, one of the few Nationally known, Black own newspaper companies, had been torched, as many as 60 people had been murdered, and the local government that was elected two days prior had been overthrown and replaced by white supremacists.

For all the violent moments in United States history, the White racist mob's gruesome attack was unique: It was the only coup d'état ever to take place on American soil.

What happened that day was nearly lost to history. For decades, the fake white perpetrators were cast as heroes in American history textbooks. The Black victims were wrongly described as instigators. It took nearly a century for the truth of what had really happened to begin to creep back into public awareness. Today, the old site of The Daily Record is a nondescript church parking lot—an ordinary-looking square of matted grass on a tree-lined street in historic Wilmington. The Wilmington Journal, a successor of sorts to the old Daily Record, stands in a white clapboard house across the street. But there's no evidence of what happened there in 1898.

Conservatives in North Carolina don't often bring up the Wilmington Black Massacre. Even many of those North Carolinians who are now aware of it are still reluctant to talk about it. Those who do sometimes stumble over words like insurrection and riot—loaded terms, and imprecise ones. It should always be known as a Black Massacre.

Not only was it a coup, though; the Black Massacre was arguably the lowest point of post-slavery racial politics. The events of Nov. 10, 1898; were a result of the long-range campaign strategy by Democratic Party leaders to regain political control of Wilmington at the time the state's most populous city – and North Carolina in the name of white supremacy.

The Democrats and most white citizens of the State feared a return to the corrupt and financially devastating rule of Republicans as had been experienced during reconstruction in the late 1860s. Waddell led white Wellingtonians in their effort to shut down a racially inflammatory Black newspaper, and then became mayor of Wilmington after the unpopular Republican regime had resigned due to the Democratic threats of being killed. As mayor, 'Waddell quickly restored sobriety and peace, demonstrating his capacity to act with courage in critical times.' He continued in this office until 1905, leading a responsible and honest government. The whole time he was nothing but a racist murderer who should have been in prison.

For something like Wilmington in 1898, it's hard to describe the level of indoctrination. In the 1910s, 1920s, 1930s, 1940s, these white people bragged about [the coup]. After that, they backed off, but it stayed in the history books, and they talked about it as an unfortunate but necessary event.

In fact, part of how historians have pieced together the real story of the Wilmington Black Massacre is by looking back at newspaper archives—from towns all across North Carolina, not just Wilmington—where similar violence was coordinated that day. They burned down Black newspapers all over the state, they shut down entry to the city from Blacks and Republicans ... It's important not to forget that this was a planned thing. This wasn't two people getting in a fight in a street corner and sparking underlying racial tensions or something like that.

But North Carolina state White Racist officials solidified their grip on power by promoting that very fiction: They originally called the 1898 incident the "Wilmington Race riot," with the implication that the event was instigated by a riot from Blacks and quelled by Waddell's White racist fighters. But, in reality, it was just a bunch of white racist people massacring Black people for living a normal life in 1898. It should always be remembered as a Black Massacre as far as I'm concerned.

Racist white people hated to see Black people in powerful positions. The Black population in Wilmington, North Carolina in 1898, was 56%. New

Orleans was 27% and Louisville was about 17%. But more importantly they had a multiracial government which was highly unusual at the time. They had Black men in positions of power in Wilmington, 10 of the 26 police officers were Black. Three of the ten city Aldermen were Black. There were Black magistrates and Black lawyers and Black doctors. The county treasurer was a Black man. The county jailer was a Black man. The city corner was a Black man. And this was as you can imagine, just intolerable to the white supremacists in 1898.

After open celebration of white-supremacist violence lost favor, a sort of bland sanitizing of history dominated recollections. That lasted until around the time of the centennial of the Black massacre, in 1998, when scholars and the descendants of the Wilmington Black community that had been nearly destroyed in 1898 began to push for recognition of what really happened. The state's acknowledgement of its 70-year reign of white supremacy during the "Solid South" period followed the same pattern. Men like Charles B. Aycock, an agitator of the Wilmington Black Massacres who three years later was elected governor on a platform of white supremacy, were revered in the state until recently—and, in some cases, still are.

But now that history is being uncovered and spread. Aycock's legacy has been reconsidered, and the collection of buildings and landmarks named after him in the state has dwindled. The Wilmington Black Massacre is widely acknowledged as a coup and as a foundational moment in creating a white-supremacist state.

North Carolina Republicans have helped uncover that history as well, although some of their acknowledgments of the legacy of white supremacy have come with partisan strings attached

great American political party is capable of subordinating the good of the nation and of humanity to its own selfish interest."

Of course, this kind of weaponization of history is most effective if the Republican and Democratic parties are viewed as unbroken ideological identities dating back to the days of Abraham Lincoln. North Carolina's own history obliterates that view. Like the rest of the South, the state experienced mass party realignment after the 1960s civil-rights movement, when southern whites began to abandon the Democratic Party.

Former Senator Jesse Helms, another Carolinian folk whose legacy is the subject of an ongoing controversy, was central to that realignment. Born and raised a Democrat in the Solid South, Helms switched parties in 1970, two years before his first Senate run. In 1974, Helms remarked of his decision:

The party veered so far to the left nationally and was taken over by the people whom I'd describe as substantially left of center in North Carolina.

And I think I felt, as many other Democrats felt and feel, that really, I had no real faith in the party. But I didn't do anything about it. Changing parties, changing party registration, is like moving from a church. But President Nixon's speech at Kansas State, I think it was, persuaded me that maybe the Republican party in North Carolina and in the nation had a chance to restore the two-party system.

After the New Deal, the Supreme Court's desegregation ruling in Brown v. Board in 1954, and the civil-rights movement, Helms shepherded white conservatives of the Solid South to the Republican Party but continued the old Democratic Party's hard line against civil-rights reforms. And his legacy still reverberates within the North Carolina GOP that he helped build.

Partisanship didn't quite move along the exact same ideological lines in the past, and both parties' histories indicate a push and pull between North and South, social conservatism and liberalism, economic orientations, populism and authoritarianism, big government and states' rights, and races. And across those spectra, politicians of all stripes have contributed to enduring racial inequalities. But white social conservatism was undoubtedly the driving force of Democratic white-supremacist regimes in the South, and its reaction to the loss of the leadership is part of what precipitated the rise of the modern Republican Party.

Whether he intends it or not, Woodlouse's acknowledgment of the Wilmington Black massacre is also acknowledgment of how that leadership was created, and that the political movement to which he belongs can trace its roots back to the murder of Black citizens and the violent overthrow of a government they elected. Lost in the fire that destroyed The Daily Record were the lives of Black citizens and the spirit of a thriving Black community, and also the most promising effort in the South to build racial solidarity. In wielding the memory of the Black Massacre in an attack against the Democrats, Woodhouse runs the risk of implicating his own party in those losses.

But history serves higher purposes than blame. It can be employed in understanding the remnants of that white-supremacist regime today and learning how to truly defeat the ills of Jim Crow. In honoring the past and the victims of Wilmington, history places the responsibility of racial equality at the feet of all political parties, and all Americans.

REFERENCE

Adrienne LaFrance, Vann R. Newkirk II. (2021, May 16). The lost history of an american coup d'état. The Atlantic. https://www.theatlantic.com/politics/archive/2017/08/wilmington-massacre/536457/

CHAPTER 13
THE 13TH BLACK MASSACRE.
PIERCE CITY, MO. 1901.

The Pierce City Black Massacre occurred on August 19, 1901, "in Missouri, when a large white mob took three Black men from jail in Pierce City and lynched them. French and William Godley, and Peter Hampton were suspects in the murder of a young white woman. Two of the Black men were quite aged and were unlikely suspects; none had a chance at a trial. These are the only recorded lynching's in Lawrence County" (1901 pierce city, missouri negro lynchings... - rarenewspapers.com. (1901, August 20).

Unrest continued, and the white mob burned five Black homes, and drove "30 Black families into the woods", affecting the roughly 300 Black residents in the town. (It had about 1,000 white residents.) Most of the Black people lost all their land and property; whites simply took over the empty Black owned properties.

This was part of a pattern of White racist violence against Black people in southwest Missouri in the early 20th century; there were also large public Black lynching's in Joplin and Springfield, resulting in many Black people abandoning the region for less hostile territory. Monett, Peirce City, Rogers, Ark., and several other towns around here have driven the negros out. By 1910 only 91 Black people remained in Lawrence County and their numbers continued to decline. The incident has been considered an act of ethnic cleansing.

In the 21st century, some Black descendants of the people who had been driven out of Pierce City threatened to file a lawsuit for the city's failure to protect their Black families and to recover the value of their families' properties, but none has been filed. There have been other grassroots efforts to acknowledge these crimes and injustices. There is not a lot of information on this Black Massacre, but I had to put this one in here as well.

REFERENCE

1901 pierce city, missouri negro lynchings... - rarenewspapers.com. (1901, August 20).   RareNewspapers.Com.
https://www.rarenewspapers.com/view/679155

CHAPTER 14
THE 14TH BLACK MASSACRE.
ATLANTA, GA. 1906.

The Atlanta Black Massacre, that occurred September 22-24, 1906, happened when Racist white mobs killed dozens of Black Georgians, wounded scores of others, and inflicted considerable property damage. Local newspaper reports of alleged assaults by Black men on white women were the catalyst for the Black Massacre, but a number of underlying causes lay behind the outbreak of the mob violence.

In the 1880s Atlanta had become the hub of the regional economy, and the city's overall population soared from 89,000 in 1900 to 150,000 in 1910; the Black population was approximately 9,000 in 1880 and 35,000 by 1900. Such growth put pressure on municipal services, increased job competition among Black and white workers, heightened class distinctions, and led the city's white leadership to respond with restrictions intended to control the daily behavior of the growing working class, with mixed success. Such conditions caused concern among elite whites, who feared the social intermingling of the races, and led to an expansion of Jim Crow segregation, particularly in the separation of white and Black neighborhoods and separate seating areas for public transportation.

The emergence during this time of a Black elite in Atlanta also contributed to racial tensions in the city. During Reconstruction (1867-76), Black men were given the right to vote, and as Blacks became more involved in the political realm, they began to establish businesses, create social networks, and build communities. As this Black elite acquired wealth, education, and prestige, its members attempted to distance themselves from an affiliation with the Black working class, and especially from the unemployed Black men who frequented the saloons on Atlanta's Decatur Street. Many whites, while uncomfortable with the advances of the Black elite, also disapproved of these saloons, which were said to be decorated with depictions of nude women. Concern over such establishments fueled prohibition advocates in the city, and many whites began to blame Black saloon-goers for rising crime rates in the growing city, and particularly for threats of sexual violence against white women" (Atlanta race riot of 1906. (2005, September 23).

The candidates for the 1906 governor's race played to white fears of a Black upper class. In the months leading up to the August election, both Hoke Smith, the former publisher of the Atlanta Journal, and Clark Howell, the editor of the Atlanta Constitution, were in the position as government officials' candidates to influence public opinion through their newspapers. Smith, with the public support of former Populist Thomas E. Watson, inflamed racial tensions in Atlanta by insisting that Black disenfranchisement was necessary to ensure that Blacks were kept "in their place"; that is, in a position inferior to that of whites. Since receiving the right to vote, Smith argued, Blacks also had sought economic and social equality. By disenfranchising Blacks, whites could maintain the social order. Howell, on the other hand, claimed that the Democratic white primary and the poll tax were already sufficient in limiting Black voting. Instead, Howell emphasized that Smith was not the racial separatist he claimed to be, and he charged that Smith had in the past cooperated with Black political leaders and thus could not be relied upon to advance the cause of white supremacy.

In addition to the political debates waged in the Journal and the Constitution, other newspapers, especially the Atlanta Georgian and the Atlanta News, carried stories throughout the year about alleged assaults on white women by Black men. The media provoked anger and hatred in its white readers—with stories, editorials, and cartoons warning of rising crime, the danger to white women of being rape by Black men, the disreputable saloons that encouraged drunkenness and licentious behavior in "brutish" men, and the desire of "uppity" Blacks to achieve equality with whites. By late September, after newspaper reports of four separate incidences of alleged assaults by Blacks on white women circulated in Atlanta, white mob violence erupted.

On the afternoon of Saturday, September 22, Atlanta newspapers reported four alleged assaults, none of which were ever substantiated, upon local white women. Extra editions of these accounts, sensationalized with lurid details and inflammatory language intended to inspire fear if not revenge, circulated, and soon thousands of white men and boys gathered in downtown Atlanta. City leaders, including Mayor James G. Woodward, sought to calm the increasingly indignant white racist crowds but failed to do so. By early evening, the White racist crowd had become a mob; from then until after midnight, they surged down Decatur Street, Pryor Street, Central

Avenue, and throughout the central business district, assaulting hundreds of Blacks. The White racist mob attacked Black-owned businesses, smashing the windows of Black leader Alonzo Herndon's barbershop. Although Herndon had closed early and was already at home when his shop was damaged, another barbershop across the street was raided by the white rioters—and the barbers were murdered. The crowd also attacked streetcars, entering trolley cars, and beating Black men and women; at least three men were beaten to death.

Finally, the White racist militia was summoned around midnight, and streetcar service was suspended. The White racist mob showed no signs of letting up, however, and the crowd was dispersed only once a heavy rain began to fall around 2:00 a.m. Atlanta was then under the control of the state militia.

On Sunday, September 23, the Atlanta newspapers reported that the state militia had been mustered to control the white mob; they also reported that Blacks were no longer a problem for whites because Saturday night's violence had driven them off public streets. While the police, armed with rifles, and militia patrolled the streets and key landmarks and guarded white property, Blacks secretly obtained weapons to arm themselves against the white mob, fearing its return. Despite the presence of law enforcement, white racist groups invaded some Black neighborhoods. In some areas Black people defended their homes and were able to turn away the incursions into their communities. (One person who described such activity was Walter White, who experienced the Black Massacre as a young boy. The incident was a defining moment for White, who went on to become secretary of the National Association for the Advancement of Colored People [NAACP], and he later described the event in his 1948 memoir A Man Called White.)

On Monday, September 24, a group of Black people held a meeting in Brownsville, a community located about two miles south of downtown Atlanta and home to the historically Black Clark College (later Clark Atlanta University) and Gammon Theological Seminary. The group was heavily armed. When Fulton County police learned of the gathering, they feared a counterattack and launched a raid on Brownsville. A shootout ensued, and an officer was killed. In response, three all-white companies of heavily armed militia were sent to Brownsville, where they seized weapons and arrested more than 250 Black men. Meanwhile, sporadic fighting continued throughout the day.

On Monday and Tuesday, city officials, businessmen, clergy, and the press called for an end to violence, because it was damaging Atlanta's image as a thriving New South city. Indeed, the Black Massacre had been covered throughout the United States as well as internationally. Fears of continued disorder prompted some white civic leaders to seek a dialogue with Black elites, establishing a rare biracial tradition that convinced mainstream northern whites that racial reconciliation was possible in the South without national intervention. Paired with Black fears of renewed violence, however, this interracial cooperation exacerbated Black social divisions as the Black elite sought to distance itself from the lower class and its interests, leaving the city among the most segregated and socially stratified in the nation.

Newspaper accounts at the time and subsequent scholarly treatments of the Black Massacre vary widely on the number of casualties. Estimates range from twenty-five to forty Black deaths, although the city coroner issued only ten death certificates for Black victims. Most accounts agree that only two whites were killed, one of whom was a woman who suffered a heart attack on seeing the white mob outside her home.

There were other consequences of the Black Massacre as well, both locally and nationally. Its aftermath saw a depression of Atlanta's Black community and economy. The Black Massacre contributed to the passage of statewide prohibition and Black suffrage restriction by 1908. It discredited for many Black leaders the accommodationist strategy of Booker T. Washington among the leadership of Black America and gave new legitimacy to the more aggressive tactics for achieving racial justice epitomized by W. E. B. Du Bois, who wrote a powerful poem, "The Litany of Atlanta," in the wake of the Black Massacre. Although it had a profound effect on many of those who experienced it, the Black Massacre was forgotten or minimized for decades in the white community and ignored in official histories of the city.

REFERENCE

Atlanta race riot of 1906. (2005, September 23). New Georgia Encyclopedia. https://www.georgiaencyclopedia.org/articles/history-archaeology/atlanta-race-riot-1906

CHAPTER 15
THE 15TH BLACK MASSACRE.
SPRINGFIELD, IL. 1908.

The Springfield Black Massacre happened on the evening of August 14,1908. Some white people try to use words like race war or riot to soften the reality of saying Black Massacre. These White people will say, "a race war broke out in the Illinois capital of Springfield. Angry over reports that a Black man had sexually assaulted a white woman, a white mob wanted to take a recently arrested suspect from the city jail and kill him. They also wanted Joe James, an out-of-town Black man who was accused of killing a white railroad engineer, Clergy Ballard, a month earlier" (The springfield race riot of 1908. (n.d.).

Late that afternoon, a White crowd gathered in front of the jail in the city's downtown and demanded that the police hand over the two Black men to them. But the police had secretly taken the prisoners out the back door into a waiting automobile and out of town to safety. When the crowd discovered that the prisoners were gone, they rioted. First, they attacked and destroyed a restaurant owned by a wealthy white citizen, Harry Loper, who had provided the automobile that the sheriff used to get the two Black men out of harm's way. The White crowd completed its work by setting fire to the automobile, which was parked in front of the restaurant.

In the early hours of the violence, as many as five thousand white Springfield residents were present, mostly as spectators. Still angry, the white rioters, minus most of the spectators. Next methodically destroyed a small Black business district downtown, breaking windows and doors, stealing or destroying merchandise, and wrecking furniture and equipment. The White mob's third and last effort that night was to destroy a nearby poor Black neighborhood called the Badlands. Most Blacks had fled the city, but as the

47

white mob swept through the area, they captured and lynched a Black barber, Scott Burton, who had stayed behind to protect his home.

The next day began quietly, but at nightfall the White rioters regrouped downtown. The new White mob marched west to the state arsenal, hoping to get at several hundred Blacks who had taken refuge there, but they were driven off by state troops who charged the crowd with bayonets fixed to their rifles. The White crowd then marched to a predominantly white, middle-class neighborhood and seized and hung an elderly wealthy Black resident. After this second killing, enough troops arrived in the capital to prevent further mass attacks on Black people. Nonetheless, what the press called "guerilla-style" hit-and-run attacks against Black residents continued through August and into September. Several more, Black owned homes were damaged, and a few Blacks caught alone on the streets were beaten by small groups of whites. The riot's toll, for a city this size, was high: two Blacks and four whites dead; hundreds of thousands of dollars' worth of property destroyed; more than forty Black families displaced when their homes were burned; and dozens of citizens of both races injured. Beyond the physical damage was injury to the reputation of the Illinois capital. The nation's newspapers carried many stories about the Black Massacre, and the name Springfield was associated in the public mind with corruption, savagery, and criminal blood lust.

Black Massacres or Anti-Black race riots occurred in northern cities were nothing new in the first decade of the twentieth century. White hostility towards Blacks was just as strong in the North as the South in this period. Segregation of the races was frequent in the North, and in Springfield and elsewhere Black People were barred from many restaurants, hotels, parks, and other public facilities. Numerous Black Massacres happened, often called race riots had occurred in the North as early as the first half of the 1800s. In the years from 1900 to 1908, anti-Black riots broke out that turned into Black Massacres in cities such as New York, and in smaller places such as Evansville and Greensburg, Indiana, and Springfield, Ohio. But not until the riot in the Illinois capital did the nation's newspapers pay much attention to these early-twentieth-century outbreaks. The Black Massacre that happened in Springfield shocked the nation and attracted extensive press coverage because the city had been Abraham Lincoln's home. The northern public was presented with the startling spectacle of whites lynching Blacks and burning their houses just blocks from the historic home of the president who had freed the slaves. Apparently white rioters understood the symbolism of their acts as well, for some reportedly shouted as they attacked Black areas, "Lincoln freed you Niggers, now we'll show you Niggers where you belong!" From that day forward, Springfield residents, and later historians, have struggled to understand why one man's alleged crime led to such extensive anti-Black violence.

Springfield in 1908 did not seem to be a troubled place on the verge of a social explosion. Apart from serving as the state capital, it was a fairly typical, middle-sized midwestern city. Its population in 1908 totaled about forty-seven thousand persons, of whom approximately twenty-five hundred (a little under 5 1/2 percent) were Black. Springfield had a stable, mixed economy based on coal, transportation, and manufacturing, as well as many businesses, such as restaurants, hotels, and taverns, that catered to the large number of tourists, government officials, and traveling businessmen that the capital attracted. Sangamon County's thirty-seven coal mines stood second only to the mines of Williamson County in production in the state. Mines ringed the city itself, and by the 1950s, all but the central core of Springfield was undercut by Mine tunnels. Six railroad lines converged on the city, including the famous Illinois Central, adding many jobs to the local economy. Factories that produced everything from bricks and flour to watches dotted the northeast, working-class quarter of the capital. Just days after the Black Massacre, a local newspaper noted that Springfield's economy was very healthy and that "there is work for all." Not surprisingly, then, no one who commented on Springfield's Black Massacre at the time blamed it on white frustration over economic hard times.

Some historians have suggested that perhaps whites believed Blacks were taking jobs away from them or were driving down wages by taking lower pay. But little interracial job competition existed in Springfield. Whites had succeeded in freezing Blacks out of good jobs in both manufacturing and transportation. Indeed, out of more than a thousand Black wage earners in the city, only four had skilled jobs in factories. As for the railroads, only a few Blacks could get work as porter's men who carried baggage on and off trains and who kept train stations swept. Skilled railroad positions such as engineers, or brakemen went to whites only. Springfield's streetcar companies hired no Blacks at all. Most Blacks were forced to take low-paying jobs as unskilled laborers, wagon-drivers, or waiters in restaurants and other jobs that whites regarded as dirty, dangerous, or beneath their dignity such as shoe shiners, janitors, or servants. Coal mining was the one area of employment open to both Blacks and whites (mostly immigrants), but it was extremely dangerous work. A few fortunate Blacks ran small businesses, such as grocery stores, restaurants, and saloons, but did not pose a threat to white shops because they served mostly Black customers. Since whites had a near monopoly on good, skilled jobs, it is unlikely that they were afraid of losing their jobs to Black competitors.

As for Springfield's Black community, no one knows exactly when the first Blacks came to the area, but tradition has it that the first settler was a

BLACK MASSACRES

West Indian, a barber named William Florville. Florville arrived in Sangamon County in 1831 and, as the story goes, met Abraham Lincoln, who encouraged him to set up a barber shop in Springfield. Florville did so and was very successful. The Black community remained very small (about two hundred people) until the Civil War. In the 1860s, freed slaves from nearby southern states such as Tennessee and Kentucky flocked to the capital, increasing its Black population by almost 300 percent. After 1870, however, the Black community grew steadily but more slowly, until it reached twenty-five hundred in 1908. It was not the case, as some later writers claimed, that a "huge Negro influx" into the city fueled interracial fight. The growth of Springfield's Black population was not rapid. Moreover, the percentage of Blacks in the city's total population had steadily declined in the previous twenty years.

In Springfield, as in many other northern cities early in the century, Black neighborhoods tended to be scattered throughout the city. Very few cities had what later would be called ghettos. No one large, predominantly Black neighborhood had yet emerged in Springfield. Still, most Blacks almost 90 percent lived in the eastern, heavily working-class half of the capital. Many of the poorest Black residents lived in what was called the Badlands: an area just northeast of downtown with the oldest, most rundown housing in the city. Part of the reason for the neighborhood's nickname, apart from its poverty and bad housing, was that city authorities, anxious to keep vice activities away from white areas, had allowed cheap saloons, houses of prostitution, and gambling dens to spread into it from downtown.

Springfield was not unusual in trying to hide away shady activities in poor Black areas: many cities early in the century followed the same policy. Poor Black residents might complain, but they often lacked the organization and political power to defend their neighborhoods against such policies. Thus, the Badlands was "bad" in part because it supported some of the city's vice industry and the high crime rates that inevitably came with it. Still, as bad as the neighborhood was, most people lived in single-family homes with large yards. Many could and did keep gardens to help maintain their families.

The second major area of Black settlement was a solidly working-class area with many Black coal miners lay in the southeast quarter of Springfield, about two miles from downtown. Unlike the Badlands, where most people rented, Blacks in this neighborhood were more likely to own their own homes. Five smaller concentrations of Blacks dotted the rest of the city. What is interesting about Black residential patterns is that with one exception, they were about the same in 1908 as they had been in 1890. Some historians have claimed that one cause of the riot was housing competition between the races, that Blacks had angered whites by "invading" their neighborhoods so often. But we now know that not only was the supply of housing good in

Springfield, but that Blacks tended to settle in "traditionally" Black areas.

The one exception to Springfield's stable residential pattern was the "Levee" downtown on East Washington Street. The Levee was an area several blocks long that included many saloons, small shops, restaurants, and part of the vice district. After 1900, small Black businesses grew up along one short stretch of the Levee, and poor Blacks began to rent small rooms above them. Although the movement of Blacks into the Levee involved only a few blocks, it may have had an important effect on race relations. Now,

after 1900, for the first time, many of Springfield's poorest and most desperate Blacks lived downtown. Their sudden, new visibility in the heart of the city may have disturbed some whites. We do know that Black ministers and Black newspapers often scolded Levee Blacks for "hanging around saloons" and for being "loafers and loud" in public. Middle-class Blacks warned again and again that public misbehavior by a few Levee Blacks might somehow create serious trouble for the majority of law-abiding Black citizens.

A healthy economy, a small, slow-growing Black population, a very low level of interracial job competition, and mostly stable residential areas: this does not look like a city on the verge of race war. What went wrong, then? One place to look for clues is in Springfield's newspapers for what whites said after the riot. Here whites blamed the riot on two things: corrupt city government and the "saloon evil," both of which encouraged lawlessness, such as rioting. Candidates running for office bought votes, and once in office took bribes from saloons and houses of prostitution. In return, politicians saw to it that the police did not enforce vice laws. Therefore, the argument ran, a large class of criminals collected in the city who did not fear the law and who would riot at a moment's notice. Adding to the problem was saloons: Springfield had too many saloons, the newspapers complained, over two hundred in a small city! Drunken, criminal Blacks were committing crimes that angered whites. The dangerous white criminal class riff-raff soaked with whiskey broke the law to take revenge looting, burning, and killing. If the city had a clean government, the newspaper claimed, there would have been fewer criminals, less drinking, and therefore no riot.

Springfield's newspapers suggest that whites were fearful of crime and disorder in the capital. And they were afraid of Black crime, too. What had shocked the city about the report of the alleged rape of a white woman in August was that the incident had occurred in a neighborhood far removed from the Levee and Badlands. Whites usually ignored most crime and violence in poor neighborhoods, even if it was interracial in nature. But the alleged rape that sparked the riot occurred in an all-white, working-class, suburban neighborhood well away from the vice district. Perhaps it suddenly seemed to white that crime was spreading into previously safe neighborhoods. Perhaps because they felt that the police were unreliable, whites believed that they had to take the law into their own hands. We do know that white rioters targeted first the two poorest Black neighborhoods, the Badlands and the Black part of the Levee. It is possible that the association of these neighborhoods with saloons and vice made them prime targets for whites worried about crime. Perhaps the worst fears of the Black middle-class had come true. But even if all this were true, though, it is clearly not the whole story.

Another place to look for clues is in the identity of the white rioters and their Black victims. Knowing who the rioters were lets us rule out old explanations for the violence and get a better picture of what really happened. As we have seen, the press reported that the White rioters were drunken, criminal riff-raffs. Historians later said they were southerners or children of southerners, that is, people with more hostile attitudes towards Blacks than northerners. Other historians say that the white rioters were mostly immigrants, especially those immigrants who labored in coal mines along with Black miners. What we actually find is that the typical white rioter was a young man in his twenties, single, employed in a working-class job, and a native of Illinois. He was not some poor riff-raff, as the newspapers had suggested, and had never been in trouble with the law before the Black massacre. He was not of southern background. He was unlikely to be an immigrant or the son of immigrants. Outsiders such as immigrants and southerners, then, cannot be blamed for the violence. It was a "home-grown" riot that turned into a Black Massacre. We also find that a significant minority of the white rioters had ties to the two whites supposedly victimized by Blacks. In fact, these friends, neighbors, relatives, and co-workers of the two white victims probably played an important role in starting the Black Massacre. For those white people, the violence would have been simple revenge for attacks on people close to them. Finally, few white coal miners rioted, even though they were the one group who might have faced job and housing competition from Blacks. In fact, the typical white rioter had little if any contact at all with Blacks: he lived well away from Black neighborhoods and worked in trades that totally excluded Black workers.

Further insights into the Black Massacres origins appear when we turn to the question of whom the white rioters targeted for attack. First, it is very clear that what White rioters wanted to do was to drive all of the Black people out of Springfield permanently. The Levee and Badlands, since they were close to where the Black Massacre began, were probably attacked first simply because they were the nearest targets. When the troops made it impossible for large crowds to form, some whites turned to threats. For months after the Black Massacre, white people who employed Blacks or who had Black

52

customers received threatening letters telling them their homes and businesses would be burned unless they cut all their ties to Black People. Even the mayor got letters threatening violence if he refused to fire the city's small number of Black policemen and firemen. Apparently, some whites thought that those Black people who had not been frightened away by the violence might be starved out of town if they lost their jobs and if white shop owners refused to sell them food.

If we look at who was targeted for attack over a period of days, an important pattern appears. Beginning late the first night of the Black Massacre and continuing through the second night and the later hit-and-run attacks, we see white rioters carefully selecting wealthier Blacks as targets. The longer the violence lasted, the more it was aimed at better-off Black citizens. By the second day of violence, white rioters passed up chances to attack the homes of poor Blacks and instead singled out for burning and looting the houses of successful Blacks, such as shop owners, barbers, government workers, and real estate dealers. Springfield's white newspapers said that rioters only attacked "bad Negroes," and that peaceful, "law-abiding" Blacks had nothing to fear. Black residents, however, knew better, and so did the White rioters. One Black woman who was a little girl in a middle-class family in 1908 recalled: "See, the people that they harmed and hurt were not really the no-gooders. They were very busy hurting the prominent, and so, of course we were frightened. We owned property; many poor whites didn't. There was a great deal of animosity toward any well-established Negro who owned his house and had a good job."

The pattern of attacks supports her opinion that Black success brought danger. The first area targeted was the Black business district. The two Blacks killed were well-off, successful businessmen who owned their own homes. All of those targeted for hit-and-run attacks were also well-off. Although what triggered the Black Massacre may have been anger over Black crime, very clearly whites were expressing resentment over any Black presence in the city at all. They also clearly resented the small number of successful Blacks in their midst.

Although the Black community in Springfield was angry and resentful long after the Black Massacre, the city quickly returned to normal. The many hundreds of Blacks who had fled to the countryside and neighboring towns soon returned and rebuilt their lives. The city began arrangements to make payments to those who lost property. Joe James, the Black man accused of murdering a white, was found guilty and he was hung. The dozens of white people arrested for rioting also went to trial, but the all-white juries refused to convict most of them. In the end, only one white rioter was punished. He

BLACK MASSACRES

was sentenced to thirty days in jail. As for the Black man accused of rape, he was freed. Much to the shock and dismay of residents, the White woman who had accused him of the crime confessed that she had lied. It soon was revealed that she had probably invented the rape story to help hide from her White husband her affair with a Black man. Not surprisingly, she and her family quickly moved away from Springfield once the news came out.

For both Blacks and whites in Springfield, the Black Massacre was a costly and painful disaster. Few it seemed, learned any lessons from the violence in the capital. Just several years later, in the World War I era, the "Great Migration" saw southern Blacks arriving in large numbers in northern cities for the first time. Many Black Massacres followed, and the Illinois cities of East St. Louis (1917) and Chicago (1919) would again find themselves criticized by the press for their violence. For all this, however, one good thing emerged from the Springfield Black Massacre. In 1909, northern white and Black reformers, outraged by the violence in Lincoln's hometown, called a small meeting. Out of this meeting grew the first strong national organization to fight for Black civil rights: the National Association for the Advancement of Colored People (aka NAACP), which has fought many long years to end anti-Black discrimination and violence towards Black People.

REFERENCE

The springfield race riot of 1908. (n.d.). https://www.lib.niu.edu/1996/iht329622.html

CHAPTER 16
THE 16TH BLACK MASSACRE.
SLOCUM, TX. 1910.

The Slocum, Texas Black Massacre happened on July 25, 1910; "in East Texas officially saw between eight and 22 Black people killed, and evidence suggests casualties were 10 times these amounts. Yet the Black Massacre has become a dirty Lone Star State secret, remarkable more for the inattention it has received than for its remembrance" (Zinn Education Project. (2017, December 7).

This Black Massacre happened because a White man named Jim Spurger did not get a job that went to a Black man, in the Black town for Black People. This White man was so mad that he didn't get the job, so he started spreading lies and rumors about how the Black people were trying to take over their towns. These lies and rumors lead to what we know as the Slocum Texas Black Massacre.

Unlike most Texas communities in the early 20th century, the small rural town of Slocum — like Rosewood, Florida — was largely Black, with several Black citizens owning their own properties and a few owning stores and other businesses. This alone, in parts of the South, might have been enough to produce violence from lazy, and extremely dumb white racist people. But in the area around Slocum, roughly 100 miles east of Waco, there were other issues, according to newspaper reports and other sometimes fighting accounts of the Black Massacre.

When a white man reportedly tried to collect a disputed debt from a well-regarded Black citizen, a confrontation occurred. Hard feelings lingered. When a regional road construction foreman put a Black person in charge of rounding up help for local road improvements, a prominent white citizen named Jim Spurger was infuriated and became an agitator.

BLACK MASSACRES

News reports, of varying truths, were reported across the country at the time, yet this history has been buried by officials.

The Slocum, Texas violence was reported (in various degrees of truth) in newspapers across the country at the time.

White Lies spread, warning of threats against White citizens and plans for Black Massacres. White racist people manipulated the local White population, and, on July 29, white hysteria transformed into a Black Massacre.

Hyped up and fighting mad by this white racist punk Jim Spurger and others, a collection of white mobs made up of Slocum locals and heavily armed white residents from all over Anderson County. Racist White people roamed through the area in groups of six or seven; or in White mobs of 30 to 40 people deep. According to some reports, some of these White Racist Gangs had up to 200 people. Members of the white mobs engaged in what authorities later termed a "potshot" occasion, firing on Black citizens at will. They moved from road to road and cabin to cabin, shooting down Black People in their tracks. Survivors of the bloodshed spread the word, and Black People began fleeing. The white mobs followed Blacks into the surrounding forests and marshes and shot many victims in the back as they fled, doing the most cowardly things a weak human being would do. Several Black bodies were discovered with bundles of clothing and personal items at their sides.

Every initial newspaper lied about reports on the transpiring bloodshed by portrayed the Black People as armed instigators, but these accounts were heinous mischaracterizations of the Black Massacre. Anderson County Sheriff William H. Black, of Palestine, Texas, and Special Deputy Godfrey Rees Fowler arrived in the Slocum area, and they discovered a terrified white populace, most of whom had slept overnight in churches and schoolhouses. But it was increasingly apparent that the alleged Black mob that had supposedly conspired to attack the local white community hadn't materialized.

When reporters gathered on July 31, up to two dozen murders had been reported, but local authorities had only eight bodies. Sheriff Black said it would be "difficult to find out just how many Black people were killed" because they were "scattered all over the woods," and buzzards would find many of the victims first.

"White men were going about killing Black People as fast as they could find them," Sheriff Black told the New York Times. "These Black people have done no wrong that I can discover," Black continued. "I don't know how many were in the White mob, but there may have been 200 or 300 White people who participated in this Black Massacre. They hunted the Black People down like they were sheep."

The truth is, a harrowing number of Black People were slaughtered in the counties of Anderson and Houston in the mid-summer of 1910. Yet today it's almost never spoke of, much less widely acknowledged, sufficiently researched, or historically considered, including its omission in A Centennial History of Anderson County, Texas (1936) and History of Houston County, Texas, 1687–1979

In every month, for the six months leading up to the Slocum Black Massacre, a Black person in the East Texas region was executed by a white mob based on allegations alone. No trials, no juries — simply white verdicts. After the lynching of Allen Brooks a Black Man, just four months prior to the Slocum Black Massacre, a photograph of his hanging body and a crowd of a hundred White spectators was made into a postcard that was mailed to White racist friends and family members. And these injustices weren't exceptions to the rule; rather, they were the rule under which Black people lived and died in that part of the world.

On August 13, 1910, a group of more than 150 Black ministers from Washington, D.C., sent a letter to President Taft regarding the Slocum Black Massacre. In the letter, the committee implored President Taft to use the powers of his "great office to suppress lynching's, murder, and other forms of lawlessness" and to do something to "make Black human life more valuable and law more universally respected."

The attorney general responded on August 24 with a shameful letter stating, "The protection of life and property is generally a duty devolving up the state authorities," and continued "Your letter and petition deal with the subject of the treatment of colored persons generally and therefore furnish no facts which would warrant this Department in taking any steps to redress the wrongs complained of."

At the initial grand jury hearing of the suspects charged in the Slocum Black Massacre, nearly every remaining resident was subpoenaed; some refused to testify and were arrested. By the time the grand jury findings were reported on August 17, several hundred witnesses had been examined. Though 11 white men were initially arrested, seven were indicted. The grand jury judge moved the trial to Harris County, distrusting the potential jury of the white peers the defendants might receive in Anderson County. The indictments received no interest or justice in Harris County. Eventually, all those white people charged were released, and none of the indictments were ever prosecuted.

In the meanwhile, the personal holdings (properties or Businesses) of many Slocum-area White racist citizens increased. The abandoned Black owned properties were absorbed or repurposed (Straight up stolen!!!!) as the now-majority white racist population saw fit. Thousands of acres of land were stolen. Jack Holly, a former slave, lost his dairy, his granary, his general store and 700 acres of land to white residents after he and his family fled the city, and this just happened in 1910.

Slocum was a prosperous Black town with Black businesses, Black homeownership, Black families. Complete Black families, when I say complete, I mean father, mother, children and probably, grandma and grandpa. That was all burnt to the ground and had to be abandoned because of this lazy, white, racist punk Jim Spurger was mad about not getting a job. The standard Southern White world order was restored.

The community reflects effects of the event to this day. While most nearby towns have Black populations of 20 percent or more, Slocum's is just under 7 percent. After, decades of effort, a marker commemorating the Slocum Black Massacre was dedicated on Jan. 16, 2016. This historical marker for the Slocum Black Massacre is important. One of the descendants of Jack Holly said, "This most definitely helps restore [the Slocum Black Massacre] to its proper place." Hollie-Jawaid continued, "It was being ignored, and by ignoring it, you're spitting in the face of those who died during that tragic event. You're basically saying either it didn't happen, or it was not important, and it's very, very important."

Despite local opposition to the marker, Chris Florance, spokesperson for the Texas Historical Society, told the Washington Post, "There is difficult history in the state, and this shows there has been a lot of change." Longtime State Judge Bascom Bentley also noted, "I'm glad the marker is there. It's part of our history, an ugly part. But the purpose of history is to teach us how to do better in the present and future."

The numerous murders committed by local white racist people and all of the Bloodshed in the Slocum, Texas in 1910 should give us all pause and spur commitments to definitively establish the truth, fully acknowledge it, and honestly and constructively address it.

Slocum, Texas is very close to Palestine, Texas, which is where the Coffield Unit is located. The Coffield Unit is the biggest prison in the State of Texas. I was on this extremely notorious prison for 12 years myself. I remember working on this unit with a Black Officer named Mr. Edwards. He was an older Black man, he was probably in late fifties, from that part of East Texas. He had a gold tooth and kept a toothpick in his mouth. The inmates called him Mr. Easy Money. I was a SSI, which is like a janitor In prison. I was standing close by Mr. Edwards, when a white Captain named Deal walked into the cell block. I watched Mr. Edwards. Old cool Mr. Easy Money froze up. He looked at me. I saw terror in his eyes. He told me get back to work. I had just finished cleaning up. Everything was perfect, and in place. I was thinking to myself, this is the perfect time for the Captain to be down here. Everything is good. I didn't understand what Mr. Edwards was so afraid of. I told him, yes sir but everything is good. He said just get out of sight. So, I did. In my eyes, Captain Deal was just a chubby old white man, who I could easily knock out in two point three seconds. But to Mr. Edwards he saw something different. After Captain Deal left, I came back around Mr. Edwards and jokingly said. Man, you be acting like you're afraid of them white folks. Mr. Edwards looked at me immediately. He came to about three inches from my face and took his toothpick out of his mouth and said in the most serious voice. He normally plays around. But this time, he told me. "MAHAM, behind every closed door, EVERY BLACK MAN. is afraid of the White man". He was dead serious. I didn't believe that we still had Black people alive who live with this belief. But after learning of this Black Massacre that occurred in the town in spent his entire life there. Bless his heart. I didn't want to disappoint him and let him know that he wasn't right. There's plenty of Black People who aren't afraid of white man or anything except disappointing God. But no man put fear of any real man. No matter what color you are. If you are a righteous man. You're worthy of respect. If you're not, you need to get your life right and stay out of the way. Rest in Peace to all of the Black People who lost their lives in this Black Massacre. Shout out to all the inmates who are on or who has ever been in the Coffield Unit, Beto Unit, and Michael Unit and all other prisons in Texas. I am a Coffield Regularz, which is a group of ex-cons that fellowship to uplift and keep each other focused.

REFERENCE

Zinn Education Project. (2017, December 7). Genocide in east texas: A history of the slocum massacre. HuffPost. https://www.huffpost.com/entry/genocide-in-east-texas-a_b_11229402

CHAPTER 17
THE 17TH BLACK MASSACRE.
FORSYTH COUNTY, GA. 1912.

The Forsyth County Black Massacre was in Georgia, in September 1912 "two separate alleged attacks on white women resulted in Black men being accused as suspects. One white woman accused two Black men of breaking into her home in Big Creek Community and said that one of them raped her. Another teenage white woman was fatally beaten and raped in the Oscarville Community. Earnest Knox was linked to the Oscarville murder along with his half-brother by a hair comb sold to him at the Oscarville store. When confronted, he confessed to the Sheriff and implicated his half-brother and mother's live-in boyfriend. The mother testified against her own Black sons during the jury trial which sentenced both to hanging. 21 days later the sentence was carried out and her sons were hung.

In the Big Creek assault, a Black preacher and his Black congregation drove to Cumming Jail to demand the release of the Black men being held for the rape of a young girl from the Big Creek Community. He threatened to blow up the town if the Black man was not released. This resulted in a white counter mob showing up in confrontation. Tempers flared and the Black preacher was harshly beaten for having been heard, suggesting that the first woman, a white woman, may have been having a consensual relationship with a black man. The white Forsyth County Sheriff locked the Black preacher inside the courthouse over night to protect him from the mob waiting outside.

Another Black man, Rob Edwards was arrested for the second murder and rape of a white woman and was being held in the small 20x20 foot jail in Cumming. He was taken from the jail by a white mob, shot and beaten to death. His body was hanged from the telephone pole which stood near the entrance of the present City Hall. In all five Black men were charged in the second crime, and Rob Edwards who was lynched by a white mob. Two youths (aged 16 and 17) in the case were convicted of rape and murder by a white jury and sentenced to death by hanging.

In 1910 more than 1,000 Black people lived in the county, which had more than 10,000 white people. After the trials and executions, bands of white racists men, known as Night Riders from Cherokee and other nearby counties threatened and intimidated Black inhabitants. These Black families fled and sold their property at discounted prices with most fleeing to Hall and Gwinnett Counties. Within the next four months, an estimated 98% of the Blacks living in the county had left due to Night Rider threats. The White racist Night Riders next moved on to Dawson and Hall Counties where they attempted to do the same. They were finally stopped when eleven Night Riders were arrested by the Hall County Sheriff" (Banished: American Ethnic Cleansings, 2015).

After the American Civil War, Black slaves in the South were emancipated and granted citizenship and the franchise through constitutional amendments. But by the turn of the 20th century, all Southern states found ways to disfranchise Blacks by passing constitutions and other laws to impede voter registration and voting. White racist Georgia Democrats passed such a law in 1908, resulting in the disfranchisement of Blacks in the state. In addition, the white-dominated Southern legislatures passed laws imposing racial segregation in public facilities, and Jim Crow customs ruled. Most rural Blacks worked as sharecroppers on white-owned land and were seldom able to get free from poverty.

The Atlanta Black Massacre of 1906 was waged by whites against Blacks and reflected tensions in a city that was rapidly changing. A Black doctor in Cumming, wrote a firsthand account saying that hundreds of Blacks were killed by whites in the Atlanta Black Massacre. The rate of lynching of Blacks by whites in Georgia and the South had been high since the late 19th century, and accounts of Black lynching's were regularly published in the local papers, often maintaining that the Blacks were responsible, guilty either of a crime or poor attitude. Black lynching's were a means by racist whites to enforce white supremacy in social affairs and ensure that Black people stayed in line.

In the 1910 census, Forsyth County was recorded as having more than 10,000 Whites, 858 Blacks and 440 Mulattoes (or mixed race). The mixed-race individuals were proof that the official ban against interracial relationships was not absolute; white men had frequently crossed the line with Black or mixed-race women.

On the night of September 5, 1912, a 22-year-old white woman named Ellen Grice, the wife of a highly respected farmer, alleged that two Black men named Toney Howell and his associate Isaiah Pirkle attempted to rape her, but were surprised and frightened away by her mother.

Within days, Forsyth County Sheriff William Reid went out and detained these two Black men, in addition to suspects Fate Chester, Johnny Bates, and Joe Rogers. All five Black men were placed in the small Forsyth County jail located near the Cumming, Georgia town square.

After the news came out about the attack on Grice, Grant Smith, a Black preacher at a local Cumming church, was heard to suggest at a barbecue that maybe the white woman had lied about the event after having been caught in a consensual act with a Black man. Outraged white racist men horse-whipped the Black preacher in front of the courthouse, and by the time Sheriff Reid rescued him and took him inside, Smith was near death.

Despite appeals by Sheriff Reid and local ministers for a growing crowd to disperse, angry whites attempted to storm the courthouse. Deputy Sheriff Mitchell Lummus had locked Smith in the large courthouse vault and saved his life. No one was ever arrested or tried for the assault on Smith.

Based on rumors that Blacks at a nearby church barbecue threatened to dynamite the town, armed white men patrolled Cumming to prevent such action. Fearing a race riot, Governor Joseph Mackey Brown declared martial law and activated 23 white members of the National Guard from Gainesville, Georgia, who successfully kept the peace.

Later that day, Sheriff Reid sent Smith, Howell, Pirkle, and the other three Black suspects to the Cobb County jail in nearby Marietta for safety. Fearing that a white racist mob from Cumming was in route, Governor Brown arranged for the Black prisoners and Smith to be moved again for their protection, this time to the Fulton County jail in Atlanta. No white mob formed in Marietta.

The police said that Toney Howell had confessed to assaulting and raping Ellen Grice and had also implicated Pirkle as an accomplice. Howell was tried by an all-white jury (Blacks were excluded as jurors because they were largely prevented from voting) and convicted in February 1913.

On September 9, 1912, a white girl who was 18 years old named, Sleety Mae Crow, was allegedly attacked in the afternoon by a Black man named Ernest Knox who was 16 years old. She was walking from home to her aunt's house nearby on Browns Bridge Road along the Forsyth-Hall County line. Knox was said to strike her from behind and drag her down a gully in the woods. Resisting, Crow pulled up a young dogwood tree by the roots. Knox allegedly raped the girl and struck her at least three times in the head with a large stone, crushing her skull.

Sleety Mae Crow's death has never been solved. After Knox allegedly told three friends what he had done, they went to see for themselves. They were Oscar Daniel, 17; Oscar's sister Trussie "Jane" Daniel, 22; and Jane's live-in boyfriend Robert "Big Rob" Edwards, 24, a close neighbor. They allegedly discussed disposing of Crow's body in the nearby Chattahoochee River, but reportedly decided that was too risky, leaving her in the woods. These allegations were never proven.

The next morning, searchers found Mae Crow at 9 a.m. She was half naked, covered with leaves, and lying face down in a pool of dry blood. She was still alive and breathing shallowly. At the scene of the alleged rape, searchers found a small pocket mirror that was said to belong to Ernest Knox. Police arrested him at home, taking him to the Gainesville, Georgia county jail to avoid the recent turmoil of Cumming. On the way Knox, after being subjected to a "form of torture known as mock lynching", confessed to having attacked Crow.

When word spread of the attack on Crow, a white lynch mob began to form that afternoon at the Gainesville jail. At midnight police officers took Knox by car to Atlanta to prevent a lynching. Oscar Daniel, Jane Daniel, and Rob Edwards were all arrested the next day as suspects in Crow's attack, as was their neighbor Ed Collins, held as a witness. They were taken to the county jail in Cumming, where an estimated crowd of 2,000 whites had formed by the time Sheriff Reid got them to the jail.

Later that day a white lynch mob of an estimated several hundred to 4,000 whites attacked the county jail. Some men gained entry and shot and killed Edwards in his cell, then dragged his body through the streets, and hanged him from a telephone pole on the Cumming town square. His body was so mutilated that early newspaper accounts identified it as Ed Collins. A deputy sheriff hid the other suspects in the alleged rape cases from the white mob. Sheriff Reid had left the vicinity.

Charges against Trussie Daniel and Ed Collins were dismissed; she agreed to a plea bargain and testifying as a state witness against her brother and Knox. Knox and Oscar Daniel stood trial. Each of the Black youths was quickly convicted of rape and murder by the all-white jury.

On the following day, October 4, both teenagers were sentenced to death by hanging, scheduled for October 25. State law prohibited public hangings. The scheduled execution was to be viewed only by the victim's family, a minister, and law officers. Gallows were built off the square in Cumming. A fence erected around the gallows was burned down the night before the execution. A white crowd estimated at between 5,000 and 8,000 gathered to watch what became a public hanging of the two Black youths. The total county population was around 12,000 at the time.

In the following months, a small racist group of white men called "Night Riders" terrorized Black citizens, warning them to leave in 24 hours or be

63

BLACK MASSACRES

killed. Those Black people who resisted were subjected to further harassment, including shots fired into their homes, or livestock killed. Some white residents tried to stop the Night Riders but were unsuccessful. An estimated 98% of Black residents of Forsyth County left. Some property owners were able to sell, likely at a loss. The renters and sharecroppers left to seek safer places. Those who had to abandon property, and failed to continue paying property tax, eventually lost their lands, and whites took it over. Many Black owned properties ended up in white hands without a sale and without a legal transfer of title. Much of this land was in the village of Oscarville, Georgia. Eventually, this village is now under the waters of the Lake Lanier. This Black Massacre was widespread across Appalachian Georgia, with Forsyth County being the third to expel its Black population after Towns and Union, while whites soon afterwards expelled Blacks from the surrounding counties of Fannin, Gilmer, and Dawson.

REFERENCE

Banished: American Ethnic Cleansings, 2015, Independent Lens, PBS; accessed 25 July 2016

CHAPTER 18
THE 18TH BLACK MASSACRE.
EAST ST. LOUIS, MO. 1917.

The East St. Louis, Black Massacre happened on July 3rd, 1917. "Drawn by employment opportunities in wartime industries, between 10,000 and 12,000 Black people left the south for East St. Louis, Illinois in 1916 and 1917 as part of the Great Migration. Many white citizens of East St. Louis, which had previously been largely white, were disturbed by this movement, and by the increase in employment of Black people in the city's industrial plants.

On July 1, 1917, a rumor spread claiming that a white man had been killed by a Black man, and tensions boiled over. The next day, the city of East St. Louis exploded into the worst Black Massacre the country had ever seen. Most of the violence -- drive-by shootings, beatings, and arson -- targeted the Black community" (American Experience. (2019, March 1). The Black Massacre raged for nearly a week, leaving nine whites and hundreds of Black people dead, and property damage estimated at close to $400,000. More than six thousand Black citizens, fearing for their lives, fled the city.

The carnage was all the more shocking because it occurred only shortly after American's entry into World War I. According to historian Winston James, "You have Black troops going off to fight to make the world safe for democracy in April and in July you have Black people being murdered in the most wanton and barbaric manner in East St. Louis; Black children being thrown back into flaming houses, people being boarded up in their houses before they're torched so that they couldn't escape. So even by American standards, East St. Louis was a horror."

At the end of a July 8 meeting in Harlem to discuss the Black Massacre, Marcus Garvey, recently returned from a year-long speaking tour of the country, asked to say a few words. The crowd stood breathless as Garvey thundered condemnation. "Millions of our people in slavery gave their lives that America might live," he said. "From the labors of these people the country grew in power, until her wealth today is computed above that of any two nations. With all the service that the Negro gave he is still a despised creature in the eyes of white people, for if he were not to them despised, the whites of this country would never allow such outrages as the East St. Louis massacre. ...This is a Black massacre that will go down in history as one of the bloodiest outrages against mankind for which any class of people could be held guilty." Garvey's speech, and a reprint entitled "The Conspiracy of the East St. Louis Riots," would propel Garvey onto the national stage.

It was also a key moment in Garvey's life. According to historian Robert Hill, "It is that speech that marks the turning point of Garvey away from Jamaica, away from a preoccupation with matters related to the West Indies and now he's not looking for support for what he is hoping to accomplish in the West Indies, but, rather, he is now sucked into the vortex of American race relations." Similar Black Massacres occurred across the country during this period, due principally to racialized competition for housing and employment. In some cities, clashes were sparked by the sight of black troops in uniform. In September 1917, for instance, black soldiers clashed with white civilians in Houston, Texas, and in 1919, during a prolonged period of civil unrest now known as the "Red Summer," 26 race riots occurred in cities across the United States.

REFERENCE

American Experience. (2019, March 1). The east st. louis riot | american experience | pbs. American Experience. https://www.pbs.org/wgbh/americanexperience/features/garvey-riot/

CHAPTER 19
THE 19TH BLACK MASSACRE.
WASHINGTON, D.C. 1919.

On Saturday, July 19, 1919, a Black Massacre occurred in the United States Capital, Washington, D.C. as a white mobs attacked the Black community and "Black soldiers returning from WWI. The white mob was retaliating against an alleged assault of a white woman, Elsie Stephnick, by a Black man, Charles Ralls" (July 19, 1919: White mobs in uniform attack african americans — who fight back — in washington, d.c. | zinn education project. (2021, May 30).

Elsie's husband was a white, civilian employee of the navy. Hundreds of white sailors, soldiers, and marines formed "a mob in uniform." Charles Ralls was found late Saturday evening. David Krugler writes in 1919, The Year of Racial Violence. The White mob spotted Ralls walking with his wife and began beating them. The couple broke free and bolted home, shots ringing out behind them. The white mob tried to break in, but Ralls' Black neighbors and friends rallied to his defense. A large and massive return of gun fire scattered the white mob and wounded a sailor. Servicemen fired back as Black residents locked their doors and prepared to defend their homes.

On Sunday, July 20, the violence continued to grow, in part because the seven-hundred-member Metropolitan Police Department failed to intervene. Black people faced brutal beatings in the streets of Washington, at the Center Market on Seventh Street NW, and even in front of the White House. By the late hours of Sunday night, July 20, the Black community began to fight back. While there were no reported casualties that night, dozens were hospitalized. The Washington Post stoked the fires on Monday with an incendiary front-page story that included a notice about a 9 p.m. assembly for servicemen to finish what they had started, an assembly that would, cause the events of the last two evenings to pale into insignificance.

BLACK MASSACRES

Black Washingtonians took the Post article seriously. They requested official protection from the government, but the state and federal government officials refused. They responded by preparing for an attack by arming themselves. When the police found out that arms dealers sold around 500 firearms that day, they shut down legal gun sales and residents turned to the black market. The violence that broke out Monday night between Black Washingtonians, armed for self-defense, and enraged white Washingtonians, many of them uniformed military men, lasted through Tuesday.

After four days of violence and lukewarm interest by the police to stop the white mob, President Woodrow Wilson finally ordered nearly two thousand soldiers from nearby military bases into Washington to suppress the rioting. The violence resulted in approximately multiple deaths [we found reports from 4 to 38 on the number] and over 100 injuries suffered by individuals of both races. This race riot was one of many Black Massacres that transpired across the nation during the so-called Red Summer but was distinguished by strong and organized Black resistance to white violence.

The race riots of 1919 happened 100 years ago this summer. Confronting a national epidemic of white mob violence, 1919 was a time when Black people defended themselves, fought back, and demanded full citizenship in thousands of acts of courage and daring, small and large, individual, and collective.

REFERENCE

July 19, 1919: White mobs in uniform attack african americans — who fight back — in washington, d.c. | zinn education project. (2021, May 30). Zinn Education Project. https://www.zinnedproject.org/news/tdih/red-summer-dc/

CHAPTER 20
THE 20TH BLACK MASSACRE.
CHICAGO, IL. 1919.

On July 27, 1919, The Chicago Black Massacre was set off by a Black teenager drowned in Lake Michigan after violating the unofficial segregation of Chicago's beaches and being stoned by a group of white youths. "His death, and the police's refusal to arrest the white man whom eyewitnesses identified as causing it, sparked a week of rioting between gangs of Black and white Chicagoans, concentrated on the South Side neighborhood surrounding the stockyards. When the riots ended on August 3, 15 white and 23 Black people had been killed and more than 500 people injured; an additional 1,000 Black families had lost their homes when they were torched by rioters" (the chicago crusader. (2019, July 26). The Chicago Crusader. https://chicagocrusader.com/local-news/85601-2/)

The "Red Summer" of 1919 marked the culmination of steadily growing tensions surrounding the great migration of Black people from the rural South to the cities of the North that took place during World War I. When the war ended in late 1918, thousands of white servicemen returned home from fighting in Europe to find that their jobs in factories, warehouses and mills had been filled by newly arrived Southern Black people or immigrants. Amid financial insecurity, racial and ethnic prejudices ran rampant. Meanwhile, Black veterans who had risked their lives fighting for the causes of freedom and democracy found themselves denied basic rights such as adequate housing and equality under the law, leading them to become increasingly militant.

In the summer of 1919, Richard J. Daley, who served as Chicago's powerful mayor from 1955 until his death in 1976, was a 17-year-old member of an Irish American organization called the Hamburg Athletic Club.

BLACK MASSACRES

Through an investigation later identified the club among the instigators of the Black Massacre, Daley and his supporters never admitted that he participated in the violence. In this stressed atmosphere, the white supremacist Ku Klux Klan organization revived its violent activities in the South, including 64 lynching's in 1918 and 83 in 1919. In the summer of 1919, Black Massacres would break out in Washington, D.C.; Knoxville, Tennessee; Longview, Texas; Phillips County, Arkansas; Omaha, Nebraska and–most dramatically–Chicago. The city's Black population had increased from 44,000 in 1909 to more than 100,000 as of 1919. Competition for jobs in the city's stockyards was particularly intense, pitting Black people against whites (both native-born and immigrants). Tensions ran highest on the city's South Side, where the great majority of Black residents lived, many of them in old, neglected housing and without adequate services.

On July 27, 1919, a 17-year-old Black male named Eugene Williams was swimming with friends in Lake Michigan when he crossed the unofficial barrier (located at 29th Street) between the city's "white" and "Black" beaches. A group of white men threw stones at Williams, hitting him, and he drowned. When police officers arrived on the scene, they refused to arrest the white man whom numerous Black people who eyewitnesses pointed to as the responsible party. Angry crowds began to gather on the beach, and reports of the incident–many distorted or exaggerated–spread quickly.

Violence soon broke out between gangs and mobs of Black and white, concentrated in the South Side neighborhood surrounding the stockyards. After police were unable to quell the riots, the state militia was called in on the fourth day, but the fighting continued until August 3. Shootings, beatings, and arson attacks eventually left 15 whites and 23 Blacks dead, and more than 500 more people (around 60 percent Black) injured. An additional 1,000 Black families were left homeless after rioters torched their residences.

In the aftermath of the Black Massacre, some suggested implementing zoning laws to formally segregate housing in Chicago, or restrictions preventing Blacks from working alongside whites in the stockyards and other industries. Such measures were rejected by Blacks and liberal white voters, however. City officials instead organized the Chicago Commission on Race Relations to investigate the root causes of the Black Massacres and find ways to combat them. The commission, which included six white men and six Black, suggested several key issues —including competition for jobs, inadequate housing options for Black people, inconsistent law enforcement and pervasive racial discrimination—but improvement in these areas would be slow in the years to come.

President Woodrow Wilson publicly blamed white people for being the instigators of Black Massacres in both Chicago and Washington, D.C., and introduced efforts to foster racial harmony, including voluntary organizations and congressional legislation. In addition to drawing attention to the growing tensions in America's urban centers, the Black Massacres in Chicago and other cities in the summer of 1919 marked the beginning of a growing willingness among Black people to fight for their rights in the face of oppression and injustice.

REFERENCE
- the chicago crusader. (2019, July 26). The Chicago Crusader. https://chicagocrusader.com/local-news/85601-2/

CHAPTER 21
THE 21ST BLACK MASSACRE.
ELAINE, AK. 1919.

The Elaine Black Massacre was the first Black Massacre I learnt about while I was in Prison. I was reading out of the letter E of the cyclopedia. I would read the cyclopedia the past my time. I never tried to learn about these things. When I would run across these Black massacres, like the one in Elaine, Arkansas. It affected me deeply. I could not believe that such things had happened in America and why I had never heard or learnt about them. After reading about the Black Massacre of Elaine, Arkansas. I wanted to learn about all Black Massacres, and I did. But this one right here was one of the worst and by far the deadliest racial confrontation in Arkansas history and possibly the bloodiest racial fight in the history of the United States. While its deepest roots lay in the state's commitment to white supremacy, the events in Elaine (Phillips County) stemmed from tense race relations and growing concerns about labor unions. A shooting incident that occurred at a meeting of the Progressive Farmers and Household Union escalated into mob violence on the part of the white people in Elaine and surrounding areas. Although the exact number is unknown, estimates of the number of Black People killed by whites' range into the hundreds; five white people lost their lives.

The fight began on the night of September 30, 1919, when approximately 100 Black people, mostly sharecroppers on the plantations of white landowners, attended a meeting of the Progressive Farmers and Household Union of America at a church in Hoop Spur (Phillips County), three miles north of Elaine. The purpose of the meeting, one of several by Black sharecroppers in the Elaine area during the previous months, was to obtain better payments for their cotton crops from the white plantation owners who dominated the area during the Jim Crow era. Black sharecroppers were often exploited in their efforts to collect payment for their cotton crops. The union had contracted with lawyer Ulysses S. Bratton, whose son, Ocier, was at this meeting. (Kenneth George Dill. (2020, July 14). The Arkansas massacre. My Life In Transition. https://kengdill.com/the-arkansas-lynchings/)

In previous months, racial fight had occurred in numerous cities in America, including Washington DC; Chicago, Illinois; Knoxville, Tennessee; and Indianapolis, Indiana. With labor fights escalating throughout the country at the end of World War I, government and business interpreted the demands of labor increasingly as the work of foreign ideologies, such as Bolshevism, that threatened the foundation of the American economy. Thrown into this highly combustible mix was the return to the United States of Black soldiers who often exhibited a less submissive attitude within the Jim Crow society around them.

Unions such as the Progressive Farmers represented a threat not only to the tenet of white supremacy but also to the basic concepts of capitalism. Although the United States was on the winning side of World War I, supporters of American capitalism found in communism a new menace to their security. With the success of the Russian Revolution, stopping the spread of international communism was seen as the duty of all loyal Americans. Arkansas governor Charles Hillman Brough told a St. Louis, Missouri, audience during the war that there existed no twilight zone in American patriotism and called Wisconsin senator Robert LaFollete, who opposed the war, a Bolshevik leader. During this Red Scare, the threat of Bolshevism seemed to be everywhere: not only in the labor strikes led by the radical Industrial Workers of the World but also in the cotton fields of Arkansas.

Leaders of the Hoop Spur union had placed armed guards around the church to prevent disruption of their meeting and intelligence gathering by white opponents. Though accounts of who fired the first shots are in sharp debate, a shootout in front of the church on the night of September 30, 1919, between the armed Black guards around the church and three individuals whose vehicle was parked in front of the church resulted in the death of W. A. Adkins, a white security officer for the Missouri-Pacific Railroad, and the wounding of Charles Pratt, Phillips County's white deputy sheriff.

The next morning, the Phillips County sheriff sent out a posse to arrest those suspected of being involved in the shooting. Although the posse encountered minimal resistance from the Black residents of the area around Elaine, the fear of Black people, who outnumbered whites in this area of Phillips County by a ratio of ten to one, led an estimated 500-to-1,000-armed white people—mostly from the surrounding Arkansas counties but also from across the river in Mississippi—to travel to Elaine to put down what was characterized by them as an "Black insurrection." On October 1, Phillips County authorities sent three telegrams to Gov. Brough, requesting that U.S. troops be sent to Elaine. Brough responded by gaining permission from the

BLACK MASSACRES

Department of War to send more than 500 battle-tested troops from Camp Pike, outside of Little Rock.

After troops arrived in Elaine on the morning of October 2, 1919, the white mobs began to depart the area and return to their homes. The military placed several hundred Black people in makeshift stockades until they could be questioned and vouched for by their white employers. (Union leader Robert Lee Hill was hidden by friends during the violence and later escaped to Kansas.) The violence even claimed those who had nothing to do with the union efforts, such as brothers David Augustine Elihue Johnston, Gibson Allen Johnston, Lewis Harrison (L. H.) Johnston, and Leroy Johnston, who were returning to Helena from a hunting trip when they were attacked and killed on October 2.

Evidence shows that the mobs of whites slaughtered black people in and around Elaine. For example, H. F. Smiddy, one of the white witnesses to the Black massacre, swore in an eye-witness account in 1921 that "several hundred of them... began to hunt negroes and shooting them as they came to them." Evidence also suggests that the troops from Camp Pike engaged in indiscriminate killing of any Black people in the area, which, if true, was a replication of past White militia activity to put down perceived Black revolts. In 1925, Sharpe Dunaway, an employee of the Arkansas Gazette, alleged that soldiers in Elaine had "committed one murder after another with all the calm deliberation in the world, either too heartless to realize the enormity of their crimes, or too drunk on moonshine to give a continental darn."

Colonel Isaac Jenks, commander of the U.S. troops at Elaine, recorded the number of Black people killed by U.S. troops as only two. In contrast, the correspondent for the Memphis Press on October 2, 1919, wrote, "Many Negroes are reported killed by the soldiers...." Other hear-say information suggests that U.S. troops also engaged in torture of Black people to make them confess and give information.

The racist white power structure in Phillips County formed a "Committee of Seven," made of influential white planters, white businessmen, and white elected officials, to investigate the cause of the disturbances. The committee met with Gov. Brough, who had ridden on the train with the troops and accompanied them on a march to the Hoop Spur area. The governor, who was reported as saying he was going to Elaine to "obtain correct information," accepted the authority of the committee in return for its commitment that no lynching's would take place in Helena (Phillips County). He returned to Little Rock the next day and told a press conference, "The situation at Elaine has been well handled and is absolutely under control. There is no danger of any lynching.... The white citizens of the county deserve unstinting praise for their actions in preventing mob violence."

From this point forward, two versions of what occurred at Elaine exist.

74

The white supremacy leaders put forward their view that Black residents had been about to revolt. E. M. Allen, a racist white planter and real estate developer who became the spokesman for Phillips County's white power structure, told the Helena World on October 7, "The present trouble with the Negroes in Phillips County is not a race riot. It is a deliberately planned Black Massacre of the Negroes against the whites directed by an organization known as the 'Progressive Farmers and Household Union of America,' established for the purpose of banding Negroes together for the killing of white people."

On the other hand, the National Association for the Advancement of Colored People (NAACP) in New York, which had sent Field Secretary Walter White to investigate the events in Elaine, contested such allegations from the outset. White wrote in the Chicago Daily News on October 19, 1919, that the belief there had been an insurrection was "only a figment of the imagination of Arkansas whites and not based on fact." He said, "White men in Helena told me that more than one hundred Negroes were killed." Famed journalist and anti-lynching activist Ida B. Wells-Barnett secretly interviewed some of the prisoners in Helena, from which she produced the pamphlet "The Arkansas Race Riot." This work also challenged allegations of an insurrection and documented the torture and other depredations the prisoners had suffered.

Within days of the initial shoot-out, 285 Black people were taken from the temporary stockades to the jail in Helena, the county seat, although the jail had space for only forty-eight. Two known white-supremist members of the Phillips County posse, T. K. Jones and H. F. Smiddy, stated in sworn affidavits in 1921 that they committed acts of torture on Black people, at the Phillips County jail and named others who had also participated in the torture of Black people. On October 31, 1919, the Phillips County all-white grand jury charged 122 Black people with crimes stemming from their own Black Massacre they created. These false charges ranged from murder to nightriding, a charge kind of like, what is today known as a terroristic threat or threatening (as defined by Act 112 of 1909). The trials began the next week, with John Elvis Miller the white man leading the prosecution. White attorneys from Helena, Arkansas were appointed by Circuit Judge J. M. Jackson to represent the first twelve Black men to go to trial. Attorney Jacob Fink, who was appointed to represent Frank Hicks the first Black man, admitted to the jury that he had not interviewed any witnesses. He made no motion for a change of venue, nor did he challenge a single prospective juror, taking the first twelve called. By November 5, 1919, the first twelve Black men given trials had been convicted of murder and sentenced to die in the electric chair. As a result, sixty-five others quickly entered plea-bargains and accepted sentences of up to twenty-one years for second-degree murder. Others had their charges dismissed or ultimately were not prosecuted.

In Little Rock and at the headquarters of the NAACP in New York, efforts began to fight the death sentences handed down in Helena, Arkansas led in part by Scipio Africanus Jones, the leading Black attorney of his era in Arkansas, and Edgar L. McHaney. Jones began to raise money in the Black community in Little Rock for the defense of the "Elaine Twelve," as the convicted men came to be known. The twelve Black men were: Frank Moore, Frank Hicks, Ed Hicks, Joe Knox, Paul Hall, Ed Coleman, Alfred Banks, Ed Ware, William Wordlaw, Albert Giles, Joe Fox, and John Martin.

At the same time, the New York offices of the NAACP, upon the advice of Arkansas attorney Ulysses S. Bratton, hired the Little Rock law firm of George C. Murphy, a former attorney general and candidate for governor, as counsel for the twelve Black men. Even at the age of seventy-nine, Murphy, a former Confederate officer and Arkansas attorney general, was considered one of the best trial attorneys in Arkansas. By late November, Jones was working with Murphy's firm to save the Elaine Twelve.

Their initial task was to appeal the sentences given to the Elaine Twelve and ask for a new trial based on errors committed by the trial court. Gov. Brough issued a stay of the executions to permit an appeal to the Arkansas Supreme Court after the motions were denied. For the next five years, the cases of the Elaine Twelve were mired in litigation as Murphy and Jones fought to save the Black men from death. They secured new trials for six of the Black men, known as the Ware defendants, based on the fact that the trial judge had not required jurors to indicate the degree of murder on their ballot forms. The convictions of the other six Black men, known as the Moore defendants, were affirmed.

The cases of the Elaine Twelve were litigated on two separate tracks. The re-trials of the Ware defendants began on May 3, 1920. During the trials, Murphy became ill, and Jones became the principal counsel. Hostility toward him was so great from local white residents that, out of fear for his life, he was said to sleep at a different Black family's house every night during the trials. The convictions were again affirmed. Gov. Brough once again stayed their executions until the Arkansas Supreme Court could again review the cases. Ultimately, the Ware defendants were freed by the Arkansas Supreme Court after two terms of court had passed, and the state of Arkansas made no move to re-try the Black men.

The Moore defendants were granted a new hearing after the U.S. Supreme Court, in the case of Moore v. Dempsey, ruled that the original proceedings in Helena had been a "mask," and that the state of Arkansas had not provided "a corrective process" that would have allowed the defendants to vindicate their constitutional right to due process of law on appeal.

Instead of pursuing a new hearing in federal court, in March 1923, Scipio Jones entered negotiations to have the Moore defendants released. To be released, the Black men would have to plead guilty to second-degree murder and a sentence of five years from the date they were first incarcerated in the Arkansas State Penitentiary. Finally, on January 14, 1925, Governor Thomas McRae ordered the release of the Moore defendants by granting them indefinite furloughs after they had pleaded guilty to second-degree murder. In the interim, Jones had secured the release of the other Elaine defendants.

Though some local white residents of Phillips County still convinced themselves that white people at the time acted appropriately to prevent a slaughter in the Elaine area in 1919, the modern view of most historians of this crisis is that white mobs unjustifiably killed an undetermined number of Black people. More controversial is the view that the military participated in this Black Massacre. Race relations in this area of Arkansas are currently quite strained for a number of reasons, including the events of 1919. A conference on the matter in Helena in 2000 resulted in no closure for the people in Phillips County. On September 29, 2019, a memorial to those who died during the Black massacre was dedicated in downtown Helena-West Helena. On November 5, 2019, the Elaine Twelve were memorialized on the Arkansas Civil Rights Heritage Trail in Little Rock, Arkansas.

REFERENCE

Kenneth George Dill. (2020, July 14). The arkansas massacre. My Life In Transition. https://kengdill.com/the-arkansas-lynchings/

CHAPTER 22
THE 22ND BLACK MASSACRE.
OCOEE, FL. 1920.

The Ocoee Black Massacre, "it's also called the "bloodiest day in United States political history." For decades the Black massacre that began on 2 November 1920 was a closely guarded secret in Orange County, Florida.

In the town of Ocoee where the Black massacre occurred, it was something the white residents didn't want to talk about. Evidence was destroyed and stories were suppressed. Something terrible happened in this little Florida town. For a long time, that's all that anyone knew.

Black families on their way to visit nearby towns would go out of their way to avoid Ocoee. They would warn their children, to stay away from that place, without explanation. According to census records, Ocoee did not have a single Black resident for sixty years straight. Ocoee was a sundown town", meaning that if you were Black, you had better not get caught in that town after the sun goes down. If caught after dark, the white people of that town would kill you. That was an Ocoee known secret (Jed Graham. (2020, July 8).

The years of 1919 and 1920 saw many Black Massacres across the nation. White mobs were whipped up by vicious rumor, political propaganda, and a healthy dose of good ole' fashioned American racism.

For the white citizens of Ocoee, it was a proud town. A white pride town. Their town was home to the third Ku Klux Klan unit formed in Florida. Two units of the United Klan's of America were nearby.

They were proud of this. They were proud of all things white. According to some reports, 90% of the town's law enforcement, public servants, lawyers, and judges were members of the Ku Klux Klan.

However, out of the 1100 citizens of Ocoee in 1920, approximately 500 of them were Black. The town was strictly segregated, and the whites referred to the Black sections of town as the Northern Quarters and Southern Quarters. This reference to quarters was enforced by the whites to remind the Black citizens of the slavery days.

Disenfranchisement after the Reconstruction Era was an effort to get around the 15th Amendment. The Democratic Party in the Southern states sought to retain their hold on power at any cost. They implemented new laws, new constitutions, and practices to deliberately block Black citizens from registering to vote and voting. Kind of like what we're seeing by the Republican Party throughout the Southern states in 2021.

In the wake of President Woodrow Wilson's support of Jim Crow laws, the Republican Party launched a concerted effort across the South to bring Black voters to the polls for the 1920 election. They hoped that overcoming the disenfranchisement of Blacks would shatter the Southern Democrat's power bloc.

The response to this effort was met by overwhelming opposition in the South. The resurgence of the Ku Klux Klan accelerated, swelling the organization's numbers in the lead up to the 1920 election. Along with the Ku Klux Klan came threats of violence and this was especially true in Florida.

Florida offered a lot of promise for the Republican Party in 1920. If they could overcome the efforts to disenfranchise Black voters, there was an opportunity to make sweeping changes to benefit their constituents.

Judge John Moses Cheney, a Republican, was running for a Florida Senate seat in the 1920 election. He also ran a campaign to register Black voters in Florida. This effort was supported in Orange County by two prominent Black businessmen, Mose Norman and July Perry.

State and local government officials knew white supremacy was in danger. They joined with the Ku Klux Klan in a last-ditch effort to stop Black voters at the polls. The two worked to help Black people register to vote including paying the poll tax for those who could not afford it. They met stiff resistance from the local Ku Klux Klan chapter. The white supremacists began a campaign of intimidation including the hanging of Black people in protest and the march of 500 KKK members through the town of Ocoee a few days before the election, on 29 October 1920.

The effort to register Black voters was meeting with success. State and local government officials knew white supremacy was in danger. They joined with the Ku Klux Klan in a last-ditch effort to stop Black voters at the polls.

Their plan in Ocoee was to station minders outside the polls to turn away Black voters. According to one account, they stationed armed KKK members across the street from the polling station. When a Black voter would attempt to vote they were challenged by the minders placed near the polling booths.

One challenge for the Black voter was, he would be required to appear before a notary public. In Ocoee, this was Justice of the Peace, a white man named R. C. Bigelow. As part of this KKK's plan, Bigelow voted early in the morning then left town on a fishing trip. This meant the Black voters had to make a long trip to Orlando to satisfy this requirement.

July Perry avoided the attempt to block Black voters by getting his vote in before the whites were able to get their plan into place. He would be the only Black person who was able to cast a vote in Ocoee that day. That morning, when another Black man Mose Norman arrived to vote, he was turned away by the minders who claimed he still owed the poll tax.

Norman then drove to Orlando to meet with Judge Cheney. He returned later that afternoon and attempted to vote again. Several conflicting stories make it difficult to discern what happened next. According to one of the accounts Mose Norman had a shotgun in his car. When he showed up to vote again the shotgun was seized by one of the white supremacists. He was then threatened and perhaps beaten before he was forced to flee the polling station.

After the polls closed a group of whites began to gather in front of the two grocery stores in Ocoee. One unlikely story heavily lied about in the white supremacists favor says that an ex-slave warned this group of white men that trouble was brewing in July Perry's house.

Further fighting stories attempt to put some form of legality upon the affair by mentioning that one of the local law enforcement officials deputized the white mob. Other accounts state the white mob was not deputized. Whether it was a legal white posse, or an illegal white mob is irrelevant since the atrocities they committed that night was far from legal.

The racist white mob then set out for July Perry's house. According to the story for the white supremacists was, thirty-seven Black men were meeting in July Perry's house. The casualties the white mob sustained, and survivor accounts make this scenario an unlikely fabrication.

The racist white mob surrounded the house while July Perry, his wife, and his daughter all Black, were inside. Perry's sons and his two hired hands were working in outlying farm buildings and not at the main house.

When the white mob attempted to capture July Perry, he defended himself. Shots were exchanged resulting in two whites dead and six injured. July Perry, his wife, and his daughter all sustained injuries. Perry, seriously injured, escaped the house and fled into a nearby cane field. The white mob pursued and eventually captured him.

According to some accounts Perry was dragged behind a car into town and hung the next morning. Other accounts indicate Perry was taken to a hospital and then to the jail. According to those accounts, around 3:30 am, on 3 November 1920, a mob of 100 white men stormed the jail and took July Perry to a light pole and hung him.

Later that morning the Black undertaker named; J. B. Stone removed July

Perry's remains from the pole. When the racist whites of Ocoee caught wind of this, they warned Stone that if he ever took down another "cow" the whites had strung up, they would do the same to him.

Other events were unfolding during the same time the white mob was murdering July Perry. A white man named Jim Graver and his Black minister Allen Franks began warning as many members of the Black community as they could of the impending violence.

The white mob sent out a call for reinforcements from nearby communities including posting it to the broadcast screen used for polling results in Orlando. Hundreds of white men responded to this call, swarming into Ocoee, armed to the teeth. They declared their desire to bring harm to the Black inhabitants of Ocoee with the most vulgar and coarse language imaginable.

Other acts of violence against Blacks began to break out in the Northern Quarters of Ocoee. Black owned homes were put to the torch, and many were killed in the fires. Roosevelt Barton was hiding in July Perry's barn. The racist white mob set the barn on fire forcing Roosevelt out of the barn where the white mob proceeded to shoot and kill him. Langmaid, a Black carpenter, was captured by the racist white mob. They viciously beat him in the middle of the street. Then they held him down and castrated him. Maggie Glenlack and her pregnant daughter, fearing for their lives hid within their home. Their bodies were found beneath the charred ruins.

Hattie Smith was visiting her pregnant sister-in-law in Ocoee when the violence broke out. Hattie managed to flee, but her sister-in-law and the rest of her family perished in the fire which consumed their home as they waited for help to arrive.

Fires and sporadic gunfire continued throughout the night, extinguishing the lives of the Black residents of the Northern Quarter. Those who made it out fled to the nearby towns of Apopka and Winter Garden or hid in the surrounding countryside.

When daylight came on 3 November 1920, the Black Massacre perpetrated by the mobs of white supremacist finally ended. The Northern Quarter of Ocoee was no more. The homes, businesses, and churches of the Black community were reduced to smoldering ruins. The only building left standing was a schoolhouse, spared because it was county property.

The Black survivors asked for permission to collect and bury the dead. The towns white leadership granted them a day to carry out the task. But the white local officials followed this with a dire warning. Flee or die.

The Black residents of the untouched Southern Quarter and the survivors of the Northern Quarter took this threat seriously and the remaining 300–

BLACK MASSACRES

400 surviving Black people fled the town, leaving behind their properties, their businesses, and their belongings. Ocoee officially became a whites-only town.

It is unknown how many Black people were injured in the attack. The death toll is disputed, ranging from 35 to 100, with the commonly accepted number ranging from 37 to 50.

Orange County and the town of Ocoee went to great lengths in an attempt to cover up this evil act. Photos of the town during this time including the destruction of the Northern Quarter were destroyed. What newspaper coverage existed about the Black massacre was heavily tilted in favor of the white supremacists downplaying the atrocity.

The town of Ocoee became an all-white community. It joined thousands of other towns across the country, known as sundown towns. People of color were not welcome in such towns after sundown.

Once the Black residents of Ocoee left town, the Ku Klux Klan maintained order around the town meant to keep out Black people. The town continued to have regular KKK rallies well into the 1960s.

Walter White of the NAACP traveled to Ocoee to investigate immediately after the Black massacre. He traveled undercover posing as a Northerner interested in purchasing orange groves in the Orange County area. According to White, the residents of the town were "still giddy with victory."

The white community of Ocoee almost succeeded in their coverup. But starting in the mid-20th century curious individuals began digging. This led to years of research and investigation by numerous researchers. Through their efforts, the Black massacre has not been forgotten.

According to census data, the town of Ocoee was an all-white town from the time of the Black massacre until 1980. Black people did not settle in the town again until 1981. The Southern White newspapers downplayed the Black massacre. And like most Black Massacres in America, no charges were ever brought against the white people who participated in this horrific event.

REFERENCE

Jed Graham. (2020, July 8). The lynching of julius "july" perry—1920. History of Yesterday. https://historyofyesterday.com/the-ocoee-massacre-of-african-american-voters-1920-268366503836

CHAPTER 23
THE 23RD BLACK MASSACRE.
TULSA, OK. 1921.

The Black Massacre of Tulsa, Ok. "Also known as Black Wall Street, which began on May 31, 1921, and left hundreds of Black residents dead and 1,000 houses destroyed, often overshadows the history of the venerable Black enclave itself. Greenwood District, with a population of 10,000 at the time, had thrived as the epicenter of Black own businesses and culture, particularly on bustling Greenwood Avenue, commonly known as Black Wall Street.

Founded in 1906, Greenwood was developed on Indian Territory, the vast area where Native American tribes had been forced to relocate, which encompasses much of modern-day Eastern Oklahoma. Some Black People who had been former slaves of the tribes, and subsequently integrated into tribal communities, acquired allotted land in Greenwood through the Dawes Act, a U.S. law that gave land to individual Native Americans. And many Black sharecroppers fleeing racial oppression relocated to the region as well, in search of a better life post-Civil War. Oklahoma begins to be promoted as a safe haven for Black people who start to come particularly post emancipation to Indian Territory" (Alexis Clark. (2021, August 30).

The biggest number of Black townships after the Civil War were located in Oklahoma. Between 1865 and 1920, Black people founded dozens of Black townships and settlements in the region. O.W. Gurley, a wealthy Black landowner, purchased 40 acres of land in Tulsa, naming it Greenwood after the town in Mississippi. Gurley is credited with having the first Black business in Greenwood in 1906, He had a vision to create something for Black people by Black people. Gurley started with a boarding house for Black People. Then word began to spread about opportunities for Black people in Greenwood and they flocked to the district. O.W. Gurley would actually loan money to people who wanted to start a business, they really had a system where someone who wanted to own a business could get help in doing that.

BLACK MASSACRES

Other prominent Black entrepreneurs followed suit. J.B. Stradford, born into slavery in Kentucky, later becoming a lawyer and activist, moved to Greenwood in 1898. He built a 55-room luxury hotel bearing his name, the biggest Black-owned hotel in the country. An outspoken businessman, Stradford believed that black people had a better chance of economic progress if they pooled their resources.

A.J. Smitherman, a publisher whose family moved to Indian Territory in the 1890s, founded the Tulsa Star, a Black newspaper headquartered in Greenwood that became instrumental in establishing the district's socially conscious mindset. The newspaper regularly informed Black people about their legal rights and any court rulings or legislation that were beneficial or harmful to their community.

Demands for equal rights were an ongoing mission for Black Americans in Tulsa despite Jim Crow oppression. Greenwood itself had a railway track running through it that separated the Black and white populations. Consequently, Gurley and Stradford's vision of having a self-contained and self-reliant Black economy came to be not only by desire but by logistics.

As a practical matter they had no choice as to where to locate their businesses, Tulsa was rigidly segregated, and Oklahoma became increasingly racist after statehood. On Greenwood Avenue, there were luxury shops, restaurants, grocery stores, hotels, jewelry and clothing stores, movie theaters, barbershops and salons, a library, pool halls, nightclubs and offices for doctors, lawyers, and dentists. Greenwood also had its own school system, post office, a savings and loan bank, hospital, and bus and taxi service.

Greenwood was home to far less wealthy Black People as well. A significant number still worked in menial jobs, such as janitors, dishwashers, porters, and domestics. The money they earned outside of Greenwood was spent within the district.

It is said within Greenwood every dollar would change hands 19 times before it left the community," said Place.

It wasn't long before the wealthy Black people attracted the attention of local white racist residents, who resented the upscale lifestyle of people they deemed to be an inferior race.

The word jealousy is certainly an appropriate word during this time. If you have particularly poor whites who are looking at this prosperous community who have large homes, fine furniture, crystals, China, linens, etc., the reaction is 'they don't deserve that.'

With the resurgence of the Ku Klux Klan, Black residents in Greenwood feared racial violence and the removal of their voting rights. The Oklahoma Supreme Court for years routinely upheld the state's restrictions on voting access for Black people, subjecting them to the poll tax and literacy tests. And

84

lynching's proliferated across the country, particularly during the Red Summer of 1919, where Black Massacres erupted in major cities across the United States, including Tulsa.

In response, The Tulsa Star encouraged Black residents to take up arms and to show up at courthouses and jails to make sure Black people who were on trial were not taken and killed by white racist lynch mobs.

But the heightened racial animosity in Tulsa erupted in 1921 when 19-year-old Dick Rowland, a Black shoe shiner was accused of attempted sexual assault of a 17-year-old white elevator operator named Sarah Page. When an angry white mob went to the courthouse to demand that the sheriff hand over Rowland, the sheriff refused. A group of about 25 armed Black men—including many World-War I veterans—then went to the courthouse to offer help guarding Rowland.

As word of a possible lynching spread, a group of around 75 armed Black men returned to the courthouse, where they were met by some 1,500 whites. After clashes between the groups, the Black men retreated to Greenwood.

A White racist mob, fully armed then descended on Greenwood, looting homes, burning down businesses and shooting Black residents dead on the spot. With millions in property damage and no help from the city, the rebuilding of Greenwood began almost immediately, thanks to the assistance of the NAACP, other Black townships in Oklahoma, donations from Black churches and a resilient Greenwood community. However, some businesses like the Tulsa Star newspaper were permanently shuttered in the wake of the violence.

The Greenwood District still exists today but after decades of urban renewal and integration the area's demographics and businesses resemble little of its storied past.

REFERENCE

Alexis Clark. (2021, August 30). Tulsa's 'black wall street' flourished as a self-contained hub in early 1900s. HISTORY. https://www.history.com/news/black-wall-street-tulsa-race-massacre

CHAPTER 24
THE 24TH BLACK MASSACRE.
ROSEWOOD, FL. 1923.

On January 1, 1923, the "Rosewood Black massacre was carried out in the small, predominantly Black town of Rosewood in central Florida. The Black massacre was instigated by the rumor that a white woman, Fanny Taylor, had been sexually assaulted by a Black man in her home in a nearby community. A group of white men, believing this rapist to be a recently escaped convict named Jesse Hunter who was hiding in Rosewood, assembled to capture this man.

Prior to this event, a series of incidents had stirred racial tensions within Rosewood. In the winter of 1922, a white schoolteacher from Perry had been murdered, and on New Year's Eve in 1922, there was a Ku Klux Klan rally held in Gainesville, located not far away from Rosewood.

In response to the allegation by Taylor, white men began to search for Jesse Hunter along with two other Black men, Aaron Carrier, and Sam Carter, who were believed to be accomplices. Carrier was captured and incarcerated while Carter was lynched. The white mob suspected Aaron Carrier's cousin Sylvester, a Rosewood resident, of harboring Jesse Hunter.

On January 4, 1923, a group of twenty-to-thirty white men approached the Carrier home and shot the family dog" (Trevor Goodloe. (2020, January 6). When Sylvester's mother Sarah came to the porch to confront the white racists mob, they shot and killed her. Sylvester defended his home, killing two men and wounding four in the ensuing battle before he too was killed. The remaining survivors fled to the swamps for refuge where many of the Black residents of Rosewood had already retreated, hoping to avoid the rising fight, and increasing racial tension.

The next day the white mob burned the Carrier home before joining with a group of 200 white men from surrounding towns who had heard about the lies that a Black man, who had killed two white men. As night descended the white mob attacked the town, slaughtering animals that Black people owned and burning Black owned buildings. An official report claims six Blacks and two whites were killed. Other accounts suggest a larger total. At the end of the carnage, only two buildings remained standing, a house and the town general store.

Many of the Black residents of Rosewood who fled into the swamps were evacuated on January 6 by two local train conductors, John, and William Bryce. Many others were hidden by John Wright, the owner of the general store. Other Black residents of Rosewood fled to Gainesville and to northern cities. Because of the Black Massacre, Rosewood became deserted.

The initial report of the Rosewood incident, presented less than a month after the Black massacre, claimed there was insufficient evidence for prosecution. Thus, no one was charged with any of the Rosewood murders. In 1994, however, as the result of new evidence and renewed interest in the event, the Florida Legislature passed the Rosewood Bill which entitled the nine Black survivors to $150,000 dollars each in compensation.

The Movie Rosewood was about this Black Massacre. It was a Rated R Movie. Directed by John Singleton and Produced by Jon Peters. The writer was Gregory Poirier and Release Date was February 21, 1997. It only grossed 13.1 million at the Box Office and the Movie runtime was 2h 20m. If you have not seen it, you should definitely check it out.

REFERENCE

Trevor Goodloe. (2020, January 6). Rosewood massacre (1923) •. BlackPast Is Dedicated to Providing a Global Audience with Reliable and Accurate Information on the History of African America and of People of African Ancestry around the World. We Aim to Promote Greater Understanding through This Knowledge to Generate Constructive Change in Our Society. https://www.blackpast.org/african-american-history/rosewood-massacre-1923/

CHAPTER 25
THE 25TH BLACK MASSACRE.
DETROIT, MI. 1943.

On June 20, 1943, The Detroit Black Massacre "started because of a fight between a Black and white Detroiters spending their Sunday on Belle Isle, the city's large park in the middle of the Detroit River. Fighting spread to the mainland, and rumors crisscrossed the city, stoking racial tensions that had been running high and threatening to boil over into violence for months. Rioting spread, with little attempt from the police to stop it (in fact, much evidence points to many white police facilitating and even participating in violence against Black people and by the time President Franklin Roosevelt sent in federal troops on the evening of June 21, hundreds of Black people had been injured, and 34 people had died: 25 Black (17 of whom were shot by police), and 9 white. Of the arrests made later, 85% were Black." (Walter p. reuther library. (n.d.). http://reuther.wayne.edu/node/8738)

Many factors contributed to the tension that was finally released during the 1943 Black Massacre. With America's entry into World War II, Detroit's auto factories were converted to manufacturing material for the war effort. As a result, Detroit experienced a large population influx of people from around the country to fill the jobs created by the War's demand. Between 1940 and 1943, Detroit's population increased by about 500,000—roughly a third of its previous population. Many of the newcomers were white southerners who often brought a tradition of discrimination against Black people with them. Blacks also flocked to the city, and frequently there was competition for jobs.

At the same time, the United Auto Workers (UAW) was gaining steam in its efforts to organize the factory workers. The UAW supported racial equality and advocated for members of all races. Despite this support, resentful white workers often called strikes when Black workers earned promotions. These walkouts over Black advancement contributed to the racial tension in the city.

Housing presented another issue. For years, Blacks had been mostly isolated in a few neighborhoods in the city such as Black Bottom and Paradise Valley. The housing in these slums was very bad, and extremely overcrowded. Especially as the population grew, people needed more and more adequate housing. In 1941, the federal government decided to build a housing project in northwest Detroit for Black people defense workers called the Sojourner Truth Housing Project. Agitation from the white community convinced the government to change the project to accommodate white tenants instead. This switch elicited an outcry not just from civil rights advocates and the Black community, but also from Mayor Edward Jeffries. The government again reversed its decision, handing the project back to Black tenants. When move-in day came at the end of February 1942, white crowds subjected the Black families to harassment and violence. Eventually, security forces were deployed in April to intimidate the white provocateurs, and finally Black families began occupying the housing projects. Many see this incident as a precursor to the Black Massacre of 1943.

While other factors such as political corruption, lack of Black representation in the police force, lack of adequate recreation facilities, and racist agitators contributed to the 1943 Black Massacre, competition for jobs and housing played the biggest roles. In late 1943, as a response to the Black Massacre, Mayor Jeffries appointed the Interracial Committee to make recommendations designed to improve governmental services that affect race relations; to investigate and address situations of discrimination and racial tension; and to produce informational programs to increase mutual understanding within the community.

REFERENCE

Walter p. reuther library. (n.d.). http://reuther.wayne.edu/node/8738)

CHAPTER 26
THE 26TH BLACK MASSACRE.
PHILADELPHIA, PA. 1985.

The Philadelphia Black Massacre started on May 13, 1985, when "the City of Philadelphia bombed its own Black citizens. Officials used a Pennsylvania State Police helicopter to drop military-grade plastic explosive from a helicopter onto a Black owned rowhouse on Osage Avenue, starting a fire that killed six adults and five children. The house was headquarters and home to members of the Black liberation group MOVE. After the bombing, the city infamously "let the fire burn" until it destroyed 61 adjacent homes over three city blocks" owned by Black people (Mistinguette Smith, For the Inquirer. (2021, May 8).

Philadelphia City Council members finally made a formal apology for the MOVE bombing last fall and committed to an annual day of remembrance beginning May 13, 2021. They did this in hopes that these steps will eventually help the city begin to heal the relationships between the Black and White people of Philadelphia. But this story does not start, or end, in Philadelphia. It is an American story, and Philly can't heal until America does. When the city decided to bomb MOVE, it followed a widespread and long-standing American practice: using tactics of war to silence, remove, and erase the existence of entire Black communities from their land. Philadelphia's day of remembrance is an opportunity for America to face this horrific pattern. It is also an opportunity for our nation to end the silence surrounding attacks by government on its own people, and to heal the intergenerational trauma that Black Americans suffer because of that silence.

Few Americans are likely to recall the facts about MOVE. A radical naturalist group, MOVE questioned the legitimacy of a government built on the oppression and genocide of Black and Native people. Its members were not popular with all of their middle- and working-class Black neighbors. Their attempts to foster an alternative political and ecological lifestyle in an urban setting led to neighbors complaining of filthy conditions and speeches amplified from speakers. The day of the firebombing, MOVE members were involved in a shootout with police, who were sent to remove them from their home by force. A handful of Black MOVE members were met with 10,000 rounds of police ammunition before the bomb was dropped on their apartment buildings.

The day was a tragedy for Philadelphia. From a national perspective, it culminated decades of American cities bombing and burning Black homes and Black owned businesses, then obliterating the details from history. In 1901, it took a white mob, armed, and assisted by the state militia, only hours to slaughter and banish the Black population of Pierce City, Mo., incinerating the homes of those who did not flee with the occupants still inside. It took more than 100 years for Texas to acknowledge the 1910 Slocum Black massacre, where, unimpeded by law enforcement, white locals executed every Black person they could find, then gave their Black owned abandoned farms, homes, and businesses to white residents. In 1912, there was the Black Massacre in Forsyth County, where white Georgians drove out all 1,100 Black residents at gunpoint, then extracted deeds to their properties from county government records as if those Black families had never existed.

And a century ago this year, Tulsa, Okla., experienced the Greenwood Black massacre, where the city deputized white residents to use ground and aircraft munitions to destroy a business district where Black people thrived, even under segregation. From Tulsa to Wilmington, N.C., to Rosewood, Fla., and Johnstown, Pa., there are many well-documented incidents of local governments removing Black people from their land through decree — or firebombing and slaughter.

These assaults were typically directed at communities of Black landowners who refused to submit to wanton racial violence and organized to fight back. When MOVE organized, Black communities in Philadelphia were resisting police extortion and payoffs, as well as excessive use of police harassment, intimidation, and shootings. Around the time of the Greenwood bombing, Black Tulsans were organizing to resist lynching.

These Black massacres have something else in common: Their stories went largely untold for decades. Local governments destroyed the physical evidence of attacks by concealing deeds to Black-owned land in Georgia or leaving the location of violence curiously unmarked, like the greensward at the site of the 1954 burning of Black homes in Vienna, Ill. In Philadelphia, unnamed remains of children from the MOVE bombing have been passed among academic institutions for anthropological study rather than returned to family for burial. Traumatized survivors around the country were silent for generations. It has taken decades for the full histories to surface. Only now have popular-culture stories like Watchmen and Lovecraft Country made the

91

bombing of Tulsa's Black Wall Street common historical knowledge.

While the City of Philadelphia has financially compensated the Black families whose homes were destroyed in the bombing of MOVE, money is not enough to heal the relationship between the city and residents. As the State of Florida learned from its payment of reparations to descendants of the Rosewood Black massacre, telling the whole, painful truth is the thing that heals.

We cannot wait another century to tell this truth: The bombing of MOVE was one of many similar incidents of government warfare against its own Black people. America's racial reconciliation requires acknowledging the story of what happened in Philadelphia as not an anomaly, but as one episode in a horrific pattern that still shapes cities, and the hearts of their citizens, across our nation. For Black Americans, officials still treat the right to own a home or build safe communities as a temporary arrangement, one revocable at any time for any reason, or for no reason at all. The hearts of non-Black people are shaped by this history too: Their American Dream was purchased with complicit silence born of terror that their communities could be next.

But Americans have the power to use Philadelphia's day of remembrance to educate ourselves. We can ask our parents if they remember MOVE, and what they know about how this country has treated Black Americans' right to safety and land in their lifetime. We can read news stories recalling the bombing and think about what government violence against Black communities looks like today. As media recount the story of MOVE, we can listen closely for the voices of Philadelphians who lived through the bombing of Osage Avenue. Their telling their story, and our listening, are acts that begin to heal trauma. We can fold these stories into lesson plans, online book groups, and government staff meeting agendas. Instead of memorializing each event — in Philadelphia, Tulsa, or elsewhere — as singular horrors, we can use the day of remembrance to tell the true, cohesive story about who we as a nation have been. If we each take on a personal commitment to sharing this truth, we could make Philadelphia the last American city that ever has to mark the day it bombed and destroyed a Black community. If we fail to remember, we will continue our amnesia of the past and the violence it brought.

REFERENCE

Mistinguette Smith, For the Inquirer. (2021, May 8). The move bombing was a philadelphia tragedy — and an american one | opinion. The Philadelphia Inquirer. https://www.inquirer.com/opinion/commentary/move-bombing-may-13-day-of-remembrance-state-violence-black-communities-20210508.html

MAHAM THE MENTOR

CHAPTER 27
THE 27TH BLACK MASSACRE.
CHARLESTON, SC. 2015.

. "The Charleston Black Massacre took place in Charleston, South Carolina on June 17, at the Emanuel African Methodist Episcopal (AME) Church 2015. Dylann Roof, a white supremacist, killed nine Black people including the senior pastor and South Carolina State Senator Clementa C. Pinkney during a prayer service at the Emanuel African Methodist Episcopal Church. The shooting increased the awareness of racial violence and terrorism in the United States particularly against Black people and led the South Carolina Assembly to remove the Confederate flag from the state capitol grounds." (Samuel Momodu. 2020, June 17).

The Black Massacre occurred on Wednesday, June 17, 2015, around 9:05 p.m. at Emanuel AME during Bible study. According to accounts of survivors who witnessed the shooting, Roof was invited in for fellowship and sat next to Senator Pinkney. Taking his pistol from his fanny pack, he first shot twenty-six-year-old Tywanza Sanders. The other victims included eighty-seven-year-old Susie Jackson, the great aunt of Sanders, Cynthia Marie Graham Hurd, Ethel Lee Lance, Depayne Middleton Doctor, Daniel Simmons, Sharonda Coleman Singleton, Myra Thompson, and Clementa C. Pinckney. The nine Black victims would later be known as the Charleston Nine.

Roof fled the church. After an FBI-led national manhunt, he was captured the next morning at a traffic stop in Shelby, North Carolina, 243 miles northwest of Charleston. Roof was arrested and returned to the Sheriff Al Cannon Detention Center in North Charleston, South Carolina. While at the jail, Roof's cell-block neighbor was former North Charleston police officer Michael Slager who was charged with the murder of Walter Lamar Scott. Roof would later confess to the murders, explaining that he wanted the murders to start a race war. He additionally told investigators that he almost changed his mind about the shootings because church members had been very nice to him.

On June 19, 2015, Roof was charged with nine counts of murder and one count of possession of a firearm. That same day, Roof appeared in Charleston County court via video conference at a bond hearing where the Black victim's families spoke to Roof and forgave him for what he did. On June 25, 2015, two funerals were held for Ethel Lance and Sharonda Coleman-Singleton at the Emanuel AME Church. Clementa Pinckney's funeral was held the next day at the basketball arena of the College of Charleston where President Barack Obama gave the eulogy. Funerals for the other Black victims, Tywanza Sanders, Susie Jackson, and Cynthia Graham Hurd, took place the following day. The last victim, Daniel Simmons, was buried on July 2, 2015.

On July 7, 2015, Roof was indicted on nine murder charges along with other federal charges that included hate crime and civil rights violations charges. His trial began in Charleston on December 7, 2016, and on December 15. He was found guilty on thirty-three charges against him and was sentenced to death on January 10, 2017; however, the sentence was later reduced to life in prison without parole on April 10, 2017. The Charleston Black Massacre prompted Black Lives Matter protests and calls for the removal of Confederate monuments and memorials across the United States including the violent Unite the Right rally in Charlottesville, Virginia in August 2017.

REFERENCE

Samuel Momodu. (2020, June 17). The charleston church massacre (2015) •. BlackPast Is Dedicated to Providing a Global Audience with Reliable and Accurate Information on the History of African America and of People of African Ancestry around the World. We Aim to Promote Greater Understanding through This Knowledge to Generate Constructive Change in Our Society. https://www.blackpast.org/african-american-history/charleston-church-massacre-2015/

FINAL WORDS FROM
MAHAM THE MENTOR

In our own personal lives', we must make decisions. One of the most important decisions we will have to make is. We must decide on what kind of person are we going to be. Am I going to be a good person or a bad person? It really doesn't matter what race you are, weather you're Black or White; anyone can be manipulated. As a 44-year-old Black man, I will say that means, are you going to be a Servant-leader or a Self-gratifier? It's just that simple. The choice is yours. The difference between a Servant Leader and a Self-gratifier is. A Servant leader knows that he's here to serve a bigger purpose than self. They will live their live Principles Over Power. They know life is not fair. They truly understand the need to be around others and others to be around them. They believe in family and friends. They look for, and truly appreciate, accountability.

A Self-Gratifier is a person who believes that they are special and loves to please and pleasure self or self-interest. These people believe that everyone should appreciate them by allowing them to continue to do them, no matter what. They believe life is fair. They care about Money, Power and Pleasure. It's Power Over Principles for them. They look for Loyalty and avoid accountability. I feel as a youth mentor for young men, especially our young Black men. I must be prepared for this serious task. I did my best to learn as much as I could before I ever tried to help someone else's child. I'm grounded in my Black Manhood, Street Smart and highly Educated. I feel that I'm on my A-game. My purpose is to keep young men out of prison, men of all races. My objective is to get these young men to become more responsible, sooner than later. That they know before the age of 18 that being financially stable means, having six months of living expenses saved up into a CD account that's gaining more interest, than the current

rate of inflation. I don't want to see young men be all about the money, but I do want them to know how to get the bag. Not to stunt on or high side on the next man. People need to understand that poverty ruins morals. Meaning that if you're broke or in a compromising position, you'll be more willing to compromise your own principles. That's a principle to work hard no matter what. There's no finish line to work.

I also try to explain to young people how some of the first signs of evilness is when people start to deny reality. This is important to me because I deal with character development. We all have negative character traits, it's easy to deny them or act like you don't understand. Most of us like to deny them and live in a fake reality. Going through life telling people that's just how I am, instead of correcting the negative character behavior that I am displaying. I did it myself, just like most people. I hated when people tried to hold me accountable. Identifying my negative character traits. Then I learned why they were trying to do it. Love! One of the most important things to know and understand about Accountability. You cannot hold someone Accountable if you do not LOVE them!!! I repeat. You cannot hold someone accountable if you do not love them. It will always be perceived as hate if you don't love that person. And nine times out of ten it probably is.

Now, back to Good and Evil. Like I said earlier I was taught that denying Reality is one of the first signs of evilness. So, we cannot deny the past and those who are trying their best to deny our Rich Black History, well now you know why. White people who are alive today, had nothing to do with the misfortune Black people went through in America. I did not write this book to shame or condemn any white person for their ancestors for participating in slavery. I wrote this book to educate my people about how we as Black people evolved up out of a very bad situation to where we're at today. As a youth mentor, I hear young and sometimes old people saying nothing has changed. It has changed dramatically. But if no one is ever speaking or teaching about it. We will never know. Writing this book was difficult and mentally exhausting. My life experiences have taught me one thing for sure, and that's I'm built for this. I am built to overcome my adversity, just like my ancestors were. So, I have chosen to make a series of Books on Black American History. Because for me to keep young men out of prison. I first must explain to them why they should love their country and know their value and the opportunity that exists for us to gain financial freedom and generational wealth. We as Black people can do that here if we stop being so easily distracted. That's why I am a big patriot of this Country. I love this country, despite all the evil things that has happened. I say that because, I know and understand life is not fair. There are 195 different countries on this planet. None of them are perfect. Despite America's misfortune, it has produced some of the greatest Black people to ever walk on the planet. The planet is 4.5 billion years old. Human beings are just 7 million to 4 thousand years old. The Year is 2021, meaning it's been only 2021 years since time reversed. I said all that to say this. We are living in the best time ever. Facts most don't know. Black people (Moors) from North Africa enslaved Spain and Portugal for 700 years, for real. Not this 400 year of slavery lies. White people were enslaved from the year 711 AD all the way up to 1492. It took military warfare to free these white people, too. Without physical combat, those white people still might have been slaves. Spain and Portugal (Portugal is also Dutch) just happened to be the first two countries to participate in the Atlantic Slave trade. Now you understand why. Can we say, Redemption?

I was taught, that an understanding beats everything. And wise people change their opinions in the presents of facts. I always figured that Black People must have invented everything on earth because Africa is the oldest continent on the planet, but I was not aware of these Black Moors enslaving white people. That explained a lot. I don't believe that we as Black people can't be racist. Now, of course we cannot implement systematic racism on any group of people. But that doesn't mean, I can't constantly stereotype white people. Attack them, whip them for little to nothing. Mistreating them, just like they did us. We as Black people can do it. Because I did it myself. I can honestly say. I did not care for white people growing up. I remember watching a Public Enemy video. And the 1965 Los Angeles riots were in the video. I remember sitting down in the Livingroom, on the couch. The music blaring. And white police officers were man handling a lot of Black people. They were being extremely rough and being unnecessarily aggressive. I couldn't believe what I was seeing. At this point in my life. I was living in Fresno. It was the 80s. I'm originally from Los Angeles, California but I had just moved back to California from Arlington, Texas. Some of my family is mixed, but the majority of them are Black. Nowhere I had ever been had an issue with my race, except in Texas.

MAHAM THE MENTOR

In Texas we definitely knew we were Black. But it was never an issue for long. Because I never tried to get along with anyone who wasn't trying to get along with me. In Fresno, there was no racism like there was in Texas. If we were in school in Texas. It's normal to say, "Hey, get that Black guy". "Tell that Mexican" or "Could you call them white boys over here". In California, New Mexico, or Colorado. Race wasn't always notice or talked about, in those places, in school, we said things like, "Can you get the guy in the Blue shirt. Tell the guy with yellow shoes on". Back to this Public Enemy video. I had to be around the age of Eight. After watching this video, I had asked my mom for confirmation on my Blackness. I mean, I knew I was Black but how Black? I knew I wasn't dark Black, but Black none the less. I said, "Mom, Am I Black? My mom said, "Yes!! Boy you're Black!!". She didn't say half Breed, or mixed, or Creole, none of that. Just, Boy you're Black. I immediately told her, that I am Black, and I am proud too. My mother looked at me and told me next. How can you be proud of something you had nothing to do with? If you want to be proud of something, be proud of something you have learned or something you've earned. Then you'll have something to be proud about. I kind of understood what she was trying to say. But after watching that video, I wasn't trying to hear none of that. I no longer wanted to deal with white people. I cut off all my white friends I did have at that time. I can honestly say I mistreated a lot of white people when I was younger. You have to be a little stupid to be racist. I am just saying, you can't be educated and racist at the same time. That's why racism is still heavy in the South. It took years for me to snap out of the stupidity. Once I educated myself, I knew that anyone can be manipulated. As a Black man. I can honestly say. I got myself locked up, embracing other people's dumb ideas. None the less, I participated in gangbanging and selling drugs. Robbing and shooting people and went to prison for it. Now, how can I personally condemn a white man for being manipulated, when I allowed myself to be manipulated by others. I knew gangbanging and street ways wasn't who I was supposed to be. But hey I embraced it, like everyone else. If I, myself, was quick to participate in my own people's destruction. Why can't these white people be tricked? Good white people were manipulated by the Confederacy. The Confederacy did not care about White people. They cared about Rich people. I understand it to the fullest. I got to meet a lot of good white people while I was incarcerated. Being around these white people helped me overcome my

99

racist overview of them all, I became friends with a lot of them. I got to understand that they are not being taught real history either. Which makes them naive to a lot of things, just like not knowing our History as a Black man will make you naive as well. That's why we must educate ourselves on our pasts so we can appreciate our future. White people are not the devil. They can be evil, just like anyone else. But there shouldn't be anything in this book that should make you want to go lose your composure and crash out behind something you discovered in this book. Please remember that as Black people. We are uniquely designed to overcome adversity.

Now, on with the recap of this book. I wrote this book because of our government, mainly our Southern State Republicans people are trying to limit the amount of Black History we teach our students. I wouldn't have had a problem with it if it wasn't for the fact. That in America, we have over a thousand different private schools in this country, that are teaching their students, that the indigenous people were just inferior to white people. And, that Nelson Mandela was a terrorist. That the biggest problem during the civil rights era was Black supremacy, and Malcolm X was the biggest Black supremacist of them all. Some are teaching that people like President Barack Obama and Black Lives Matter are the actual reasons for the racism in this country. Some are teaching that slave owners, were just plantation owners. And that slaves were just plantation workers. Some of these white people are trying to completely take white supremacy out of the equation. Some white people are trying to rewrite history so that it doesn't make white people look bad, and by doing so, it makes the Black people that were affected the most, negatively, look like the bad people. And we can't have that.

Black Massacres were occurring all across America after the Civil War started. Most of these Black Massacres were behind the Black vote. Whenever I hear a Black person say, I don't believe my vote counts, I'll always ask them if they believe in the KKK or their existence? Because if you do believe that they were real racist white people, that rode horses and wore sheets over their heads and terrorize Black people. What were they doing it for? It was to discourage us from voting. Now, in 2021, we really don't need the KKK anymore, especially when we have plenty of Black People doing a great job convincing Black people to not vote by constantly saying, our vote doesn't count. Just remember, if your vote doesn't count or doesn't matter, why was there a KKK in the first place or all these Black Massacres. Let that sink in.

Black Massacres started popping up immediately after the Civil War started. Racist White Supremist were involved in all of them. From 1863 to 1963, 100 years of real racist white people terrorized Black people because of the fear of losing power and being held accountable one day, for the evilness they put off into the world. This book was a sad and dark one. But it was absolutely necessary. As voter suppression and limiting Black American History is real. Republicans are doing it again. The irony is the Republicans hate the Democrats so much but are following the old Democratic play book. After the Civil War, three amendments were added to the United States Constitution. The last one gave Black men the Right to vote. Racist White people have been trying to suppress the Black vote since day one. In 2021, I am seeing some of the same voter suppression tactics and the white washing history. Trying to limit Critical Race Theories is not new. Most of the Black Massacres you just read won't be in your school text books.

As 2021 goes and fades away. So will our Black History if we don't do anything about it. Thank you for taking the time to read my book. I personally struggled with education. I can still remember being grown and reading at a 4th grade reading level. Now, I'm writing books. All I can say is, it's an evolution, not a revolution. If you knew better, then you can do better. The more you know, the less you can be manipulated by someone else, even me.

Maham the Mentor.

ABOUT THE AUTHOR

Maham the Mentor also known as Phillip (Kevin) DuBriel was born April 29, 1977, with his twin in Los Angeles. His biological father (Black Male) was murdered on New Year's Eve of 1977, almost five months before he was born. His biological mother (White Female) was found dead from a drug overdose October 9th, 1977, just four months after he was born. Leaving behind his sister, brothers, and himself. His parents' personal lifestyle led them to their deaths, and they were all put up for adoption.

Maham the Mentor and his twin were separated from the rest of his siblings in hopes that they would be adopted faster. They were moved through seven different foster homes before they were adopted by the DuBriel family consisting of Marsha Metoyer (Creole/ Black) and John DuBriel (Creole/ Black), Maham the Mentor was one year old. At the time of his adoption, the DuBriels lived in Long Beach, but moved to Albuquerque, New Mexico while he was still a baby. The DuBriels were good parents; they taught him right from wrong and the importance of family values. There was a lot of family there and there was a lot of love. Moving was normal for the DuBriel family. At five he moved to Colorado Springs, Colorado. Where he lived was nice, great people, real cold, snowed a lot, but no family. His parents got a divorce when he was seven; he was still living in Colorado Springs at the time. With only his mother and twin they moved to Arlington, Texas. Life in Texas was not as good as other places he had lived. The environment in Arlington was oozing with racism. Most people did not even know they were being racist, it was just normal for them. He did not live in Texas long, at nine, he moved to Fresno. Back in California again. He had plenty of family there, but none in Fresno. Maham the Mentor's first job was delivering the Fresno Bee (newspaper). He only stayed there for a couple of years, too. At about 10, he moved to Marksville, Louisiana. Talking about a culture shock, He was a city boy and Marksville was extremely country. He learned to appreciate the openness. It was nice and he seemed to be related to everybody in that part of Louisiana. Louisiana did not last, either. At 11 he moved to Dallas, by this time, he was just starting the sixth grade. His mom now had a live-in boyfriend name Michael (Black Male).

Maham the Mentor, as a child, could be a good kid but he stayed into trouble, moving so much. He learned how to make friends easily, being tough. He was always well liked and had plenty of friends. He was also a great athlete. In school he was always behind because he moved so much. he was a poor student except math and P.E. In Jr. High he failed most of everything. he started passing classes in high school, because his stepmother told him, he

102

wasn't smart enough to pass anything and that he should drop-out and get a job. Passing allowed him to play sports, he was good in everything. The last grade he completed was the eleventh; he was sent to prison while he was still in the twelfth grade, and he just was 18.

Maham the Mentor started getting into trouble when he moved to Dallas. His mom's new boyfriend, Michael was the worst thing that could have happened to him. He hated everything about him, and he hated him back. They fought all the time, and he was only 12. He hated being home, so he stayed in the streets as much as possible. His neighborhood at that time was full of gangs. Gangbanging was a normal way of life in this time and era, especially in that part of the city, and he, at that time, was no different than anybody else.

Maham the Mentor joined a little gang call BGP at 12 and did all the gangbanging stuff. Life as a gangster, did not last too long. In his apartment complex, he was shot in a gang shoot-out by another gang member and then pistol-whipped by a couple of Dallas Police officers, all in the same night. He was only 13. They moved to a different neighborhood in Dallas. His new neighborhood was not gang infested like the last one, but what it lacked in gang activity, it made up in drug activity. It was never his intentions to get involved in anything drug related, but it was not long before selling drugs seemed extremely attractive to him. Selling drugs was something he became good at, and he made plenty of money doing it. Gangbanging and selling drugs had pretty much ruined his consciousness. He only cared about his family, his so-called friends, and his neighborhood. He was a nightmare to anyone who crossed him. Breaking the law was normal for him; he sold drugs daily, robbed and shot at people occasionally. He was known in the neighborhood for being a good friend or your worst enemy.

Maham the Mentor did not drink alcohol or use any drugs. He hated cigarettes, but he started smoking weed when he was around 18. While still in high school, he caught an Aggravated Robbery with a deadly weapon and an Attempt Murder case and was sentenced to 15 in prison. He went in and came out in one piece. He ended up doing 10 years and nine months on that 15. Once out, he was getting his life back on track, but the world as he knew it would change again. Fresh out of prison, he was doing great, then BAM! His dad died from a massive heart attack while trying to come see him. Words cannot fully explain the pain he felt when his dad died. He had been working hard so his dad could be proud of him and now his dad was gone. His dad was one of his biggest supporters. His lost caused him to lose focus of his priorities, He soon found himself back in prison, with two drug related cases and a gun charge.

Maham the Mentor true transformation came on his second trip to prison. His criminal history, along with his new changes, made him look like he deserved a Life sentence. He had now hit the lowest point in his life, and he finally felt it was necessary to ask God for help. He did not wish to be free, but he asked God to give him something he could do, something reasonable. He promised God, if he blessed him with the opportunity to walk as a free man again, he would be a testament to His power. He ended up getting three eight-year sentences, all running concurrently. God did His part and now he wanted to his part. He noticed when he was free, all employers wanted people with computer skills. So, once in prison, He signed up for computer classes to improve self, educationally. When he was finally called to the Education Dept. to talk to the school counselor about taking Business Computer Information System (BCIS) classes, he found out that he could go to college under a grant but couldn't go to college without taking the THEA test. But his Educational Average (EA) score was 9.9 (too low), and it had to be at least an 11.0. He started BCIS, studied, and retook the EA test and made a 12.1. He then took and passed the THEA test and began college. He went to college while taking six hours (six months courses) BCIS and Computer Information Technology (C.I.T.). He maintained a 4.0 GPA in both trade courses earning 24 college credits for C.I.T. September 2012; he became the first person in his immediate family to graduate from college. He graduated from Trinity Valley Community College (TVCC) with honors in Applied Science for CIT and Horticulture; He maintained an "overall" 3.72 GPA with 92 credited hours. The first trip to prison He stayed in trouble (G4), now, His second trip, he was an outside trustee (G1) for over three years.

Maham the Mentor life has been extremely unique so far. He has had a lot of good times and a lot of bad times, but he has never given up on himself. His experiences have turned him into a very serious person, with a very positive attitude about his future. He knows, that if he puts his mind to it, nothing is impossible. Before becoming aware that he wanted to be a mentor. He was already studying to be an entrepreneur and learning about business and accounting.

Maham the Mentor was paroled out of prison in 2014. He immediately helped his twin brother with starting his own company called Superior Wash, a Truck washing service business in Memphis, TN. It took a couple of years, but the business has been successful and steady growing. Maham the Mentor was fully discharged from ALL Criminal Cases in 2016. He lives a free life as a Mentor, Servant-Leader, Entrepreneur, truck driver and brother. He lives in Castle Hills in Carrollton, Tx. He is the Founder and Executive Director of the Society of Is-Real. A Youth Development

Organization. And he's also a volunteer for numerous non-profit organizations like the MOF (Miles of Freedom) organization, who helps Ex-offenders getting out of prison. And the PEP (Prison Entrepreneurship Program) which he won #1 Entrepreneur in his class, helps ex-offenders transform back into to society from prison and starting businesses. And OGU (Original Gangster University), which is all about stopping the violence in the Dallas and other cities around the Nation.

You can find more about Maham the Mentor at
www.mahamthementor.com